The Anti-Gnostic Fathers

*Early Christian Polemics Against
'Hidden Knowledge'*

*Tertullian, Irenaeus, and
the Fight to Preserve Orthodoxy*

A Modern Translation

Adapted for the Contemporary Reader

Various Church Fathers

Translated by Tim Zengerink

© **Copyright 2025**
All rights reserved.

It is not legal to reproduce, duplicate, or transmit any part of this document in either electronic means or in printed format. Recording of this publication is strictly prohibited and any storage of this document is not allowed unless with written permission from the publisher except for the use of brief quotations in a book review.

This book contains works of fiction. Any resemblance to persons living or dead, or places, events, or locations is purely coincidental.

Table of Contents

Preface - Message to the Reader 1

Introduction 4

Epistle of the Apostles 8

Irenaeus – Against Heresies (Selections) 13

    Chapter I 14

    Chapter II 16

    Chapter III 18

    Chapter IV 20

    Chapter V 23

    Chapter VI 26

    Chapter VII 29

    Chapter VIII 31

    Chapter IX 35

    Chapter X 38

    Chapter XI 40

    Chapter XII 43

    Chapter XIII 45

    Chapter XIV 48

    Chapter XV 52

    Chapter XVI 55

    Chapter XVII 58

    Chapter XVIII 59

    Chapter XIX 62

    Chapter XX 63

    Chapter XXI 65

Chapter XXII 68
Chapter XXIII 69
Chapter XXIV 71
Chapter XXV 74
Chapter XXVI 76
Chapter XXVII 78
Chapter XXVIII 79
Chapter XXIX 81
Chapter XXX 83
Chapter XXXI 90
Thank You for Reading 93

Preface - Message to the Reader

What If You Could Help Rebuild the Greatest Library in Human History?

Thousands of years ago, the Library of Alexandria stood as the crown jewel of human achievement — a sanctuary where the collected wisdom of every known civilization was gathered, preserved, and shared freely.

And then, it was lost.

Through fire, conquest, and the slow erosion of time, humanity lost not just books — but ideas, dreams, discoveries, and stories that could have changed the world forever.

Today, the Library of Alexandria lives again — and you are invited to be a part of its restoration.

Our mission is simple yet profound:

To rebuild the greatest library the world has ever known, and to translate all timeless works into every language and dialect, so that no seeker of knowledge is ever left behind again.

By joining our movement to rebuild the modern Library of Alexandria, you become part of an unprecedented mission:

- **Unlimited Access to the Greatest Audiobooks & eBooks Ever Written:**
  Instantly explore thousands of legendary works—Plato, Shakespeare, Jane Austen, Leo Tolstoy, and countless more. All

instantly available to read or listen, placing a complete literary universe at your fingertips.

- **Beautiful Paperback & Deluxe Editions at Printing Cost**

   Own any title as an elegant paperback, deluxe hardcover, or stunning collectible boxset—offered to you at true printing cost, delivered straight to your door. Build your personal Library of Alexandria, crafted for beauty, built for durability, and worthy of proud display.

- **Fresh Translations for Modern Readers—in Every Language & Dialect**

   Enjoy timeless masterpieces reimagined in clear, contemporary language—no more outdated phrases or obscure references. Alongside the original versions, we're tirelessly translating these classics into every language and dialect imaginable, ensuring accessibility and understanding across cultures and generations.

- **Join a Global Renaissance of Literature & Knowledge**

   You directly support expanding our library, publishing deluxe editions at true cost, translating works into all global languages, and bringing humanity's greatest stories to people everywhere. By joining today, you're not just preserving a legacy of masterpieces; you set in motion a powerful wave of literary accessibility.

Become a Torchbearer of Knowledge.

Join us for free now at **LibraryofAlexandria.com**

Together, we will ensure that the light of human wisdom never fades again.

With gratitude and a shared love of knowledge,
The Modern Library of Alexandria Team

Visit:

www.libraryofalexandria.com

Or scan the code below:

Introduction

Gnosticism and the Crisis of Early Christianity

In the first few centuries following the death and resurrection of Jesus, Christianity was anything but doctrinally unified. Diverse theological strands emerged across the Mediterranean, each offering a unique interpretation of who Jesus was, what salvation meant, and how believers ought to relate to the divine. Among the most potent of these rivals to what would become mainstream orthodoxy was Gnosticism—a complex and often esoteric movement that presented alternative views on creation, redemption, and the nature of God. To the Gnostics, salvation was not granted by faith alone or through Christ's atoning death in a traditional sense. Instead, it was attained through secret knowledge (gnōsis), revealing the hidden truths of existence and the divine.

In the face of this growing challenge, a cadre of early Christian thinkers emerged to confront and refute what they deemed dangerous heresies. Chief among them were Irenaeus of Lyons, Tertullian of Carthage, and Hippolytus of Rome. These church fathers were not merely theologians; they were also polemicists, apologists, and, in a sense, historians. Through detailed arguments and systematic rebuttals, they sought to expose the inconsistencies and theological dangers of Gnostic thought while affirming the foundational principles of apostolic Christianity.

Their writings form a vital bridge between the apostolic age and the era of conciliar orthodoxy, shaping what would become the boundaries of Christian belief. But more than that, these works offer a window into the intellectual and spiritual ferment of early Christianity—a time when the identity of the Church, the meaning of Christ, and the canon of Scripture were all in active dispute.

Mapping the Heresies: Irenaeus, Tertullian, and Hippolytus

The battle against Gnosticism was fought on several fronts, each with its own strategies and targets. Irenaeus of Lyons, writing in the late second century, produced his seminal work Against Heresies (Adversus Haereses) not only to dismantle the labyrinthine speculations of Valentinus and his followers but also to lay out a coherent vision of Christian orthodoxy rooted in apostolic tradition. For Irenaeus, the Church's unity was inseparable from its doctrine. Scripture, rightly interpreted through the apostolic rule of faith, was the key to countering Gnostic distortions.

Tertullian, a fiery North African convert and skilled rhetorician, brought legal precision and philosophical acuity to the theological battlefield. In Adversus Marcionem, he dismantled the dualistic worldview of Marcion, who rejected the Old Testament and portrayed the God of Jesus as entirely separate from the Creator God of Genesis. In Adversus Valentinianos, Tertullian turned his satire and logic against the self-styled elite who claimed privileged access to divine mysteries. Tertullian's insistence on the authority of the Church, the coherence of Scripture, and the embodied nature of Christ challenged the disembodied, speculative spirituality of the Gnostics.

Hippolytus, a Roman theologian and presbyter, carried this intellectual resistance further in his massive compendium, Refutation of All Heresies. Aimed at a wide array of heretical groups, his work is especially valuable for preserving quotations and doctrines from now-lost Gnostic texts and sects. Hippolytus believed that these teachings were not merely misguided but dangerously deceptive, and he traced their roots to pre-Christian philosophies and esoteric mystery religions. His catalog of heresies is as much an anthropological record as it is a theological polemic.

While each father had his own approach and emphasis, they shared several key commitments: the importance of apostolic succession, the unity of Scripture, and the bodily incarnation, crucifixion, and resurrection of Jesus. They rejected Gnostic docetism—the belief that Christ only appeared to be human—as a denial of both divine love and the redemptive purpose of material creation. For the anti-Gnostic fathers, to deny Christ's true humanity was to sever the very bridge between God and humankind.

The Legacy of the Anti-Gnostic Fathers

The writings contained in this volume were not merely theological exercises—they were acts of preservation. In defining what Christianity was not, the anti-Gnostic fathers helped to articulate what Christianity was. Their polemics sharpened the contours of doctrine, shaping the early creeds and canon. But they also did more: they revealed the deep spiritual questions and anxieties of their age. The Gnostics were not fringe mystics with bizarre ideas; they were deeply engaged thinkers wrestling with the problem of evil, the nature of God, and the fate of the soul. That they came to different conclusions than the emerging orthodoxy should not blind us to the seriousness of their concerns—or the brilliance of their insights.

Indeed, it is partly thanks to these church fathers that we possess as much information about Gnostic beliefs as we do. Their refutations often included detailed summaries of Gnostic cosmologies, mythologies, and rituals—information not always preserved in Gnostic sources themselves. Irenaeus, Tertullian, and Hippolytus may have written to refute, but they also documented.

In the modern age, as interest in Gnostic texts such as those found at Nag Hammadi resurges, the writings of the anti-Gnostic fathers take on renewed relevance. They are not merely reactionary voices from a distant past but thoughtful participants in an ancient and ongoing dialogue about truth, authority, and the human quest for the divine.

This edition offers selections from these foundational figures, adapted into contemporary language for accessibility while preserving their polemical force and historical significance. It is an invitation not only to understand the early Church's theological battles but to appreciate the enduring value of doctrinal clarity, intellectual rigor, and spiritual conviction. Whether one agrees with their conclusions or not, the anti-Gnostic fathers stand as towering figures who helped define the boundaries of the Christian faith—and in doing so, shaped the course of Western religious history.

Epistle of the Apostles

Acts Of Peter And The Twelve Apostles

We were called to complete our mission, working together as the Lord planned. We made a promise to one another and prepared ourselves for what was ahead.

At the right moment, guided by the Lord, we went down to the sea and found a ship waiting at the shore, ready to sail. We spoke to the sailors, asking if we could join them, and they welcomed us warmly, as if it had been arranged by God. After we boarded, we sailed for a full day and night. Then, a wind rose behind us, pushing the ship toward a small city in the middle of the sea.

When we arrived at the dock, I, Peter, asked one of the locals for the name of the city. He replied, "This city is called Habitation, which means Foundation and Endurance." Near the dock, a man stood holding a palm branch. After unloading our things, I went into the city to find a place for us to stay.

As I searched, I saw a man walking toward me. He was dressed in a cloth tied around his waist with a gold belt, and a napkin covered his chest, shoulders, head, and hands. He looked striking—tall and beautiful. I noticed four parts of him: the soles of his feet, part of his chest, the palms of his hands, and his face. In his left hand, he held something like a book cover, and in his right hand, he carried a staff made of styrax wood. His voice was strong as he called out, "Pearls! Pearls!"

I assumed he was a local and called out, "My brother and my friend!" He answered, "You are right to call me that. What do you seek from me?" I told him, "I am looking for a place to stay for myself and my companions, as we are strangers here." He responded, "That is why I called you my brother and friend, for I too am a stranger like you."

Then he continued calling out, "Pearls! Pearls!" Rich men of the city heard him and came out from their storage rooms or looked down from their upper windows. Seeing that he carried no bag or goods, they assumed he was mocking them and returned to their homes.

But the poor people of the city heard him and came forward, saying, "Please show us the pearl so we can see it with our own eyes. We are poor and cannot afford to buy it, but we want to see it and tell others about it." He replied, "If you truly want to see it, come to my city. There, I will not only show you the pearl but give it to you for free."

The poor were surprised and said, "We are beggars. No one gives pearls to beggars—only bread or small coins. Show us the pearl here so we can proudly tell our friends we have seen one. Pearls are not something people like us ever get to see." Again, he said, "If you truly desire it, come to my city, where I will show it to you and give it to you freely." Hearing this, the poor and beggars were filled with joy.

Later, some men asked Peter about the challenges they might face. Peter shared stories he had heard, explaining the difficulties of their mission and the struggles they would encounter on their journey.

Peter then turned to the man selling the pearl and said, "I want to know your name and what dangers lie on the road to your city. We are servants of God, called to spread His word wherever we go." The man replied, "My name is Lithargoel, which means 'the light, like a gazelle.'

"As for the road to my city, no one can travel it unless they leave behind everything they own and fast every day along the way. The path is dangerous, full of robbers and wild animals. Those who carry bread will be attacked by black dogs. Those dressed in fine clothing will be robbed and killed. Anyone carrying water will be hunted by thirsty wolves. And those who worry about meat or vegetables will be eaten by lions, or, if they escape the lions, they will be trampled by bulls."

When he said these words, I sighed deeply and thought, "This journey is full of challenges! I wish Jesus would give us the strength to walk this path!" He noticed my concern and asked, "Why are you troubled if you truly know the name of Jesus and believe in him? He has great power to give strength. I also believe in the Father who sent him."

I asked, "What is the name of the city you are going to?" He replied, "My city is called 'Nine Gates.' Let us praise God as we remember that the tenth gate is the head." After saying this, he left, and I continued on my way in peace.

As I was about to call my friends, I saw waves and tall walls surrounding the city. The sight amazed me. I noticed an old man sitting nearby and asked if this city was truly called Habitation. He replied, "Yes, it is called Habitation." Then he explained, "We live here because we endure."

I said, "This name is fitting because it is through endurance that cities thrive and great kingdoms are built. Those who endure hardships in faith will live in the kingdom of heaven."

I hurried to gather my friends so we could go to the city that Lithargoel had spoken about. Together, in faith, we gave up everything, just as he had instructed. We avoided the robbers because we carried nothing of value. We escaped the wolves because we had no water for them to crave. We passed by the lions unharmed because we had no meat with us, and the bulls did not attack us because we carried no vegetables.

A deep sense of joy and peace, like the peace of our Lord, filled us. We rested at the city gate, talking about faith instead of worldly matters. As we reflected on the dangers we had avoided, Lithargoel appeared again. This time, he looked like a doctor carrying a box of ointments, followed by a young disciple with a bag of medicine. We did not recognize him.

Peter spoke to him, saying, "Please help us, as we are strangers. Take us to the house of Lithargoel before night falls." The man replied, "I will show you the way with a sincere heart. But tell me, how do you know this good man? He does not reveal himself to everyone, for he is the son of a great king. Wait here while I go tend to a man who needs healing. I will return soon." He hurried away but soon came back.

When he returned, he called out, "Peter!" Peter was startled and asked, "How do you know my name?" Lithargoel replied, "Who gave you the name Peter?" Peter answered, "Jesus Christ, the Son of the living God, gave me this name." Lithargoel then said, "It is I. Recognize me, Peter." He removed his disguise, revealing his true identity.

We fell to the ground and worshiped him. There were eleven of us, and he stretched out his hand to help us up. We spoke humbly, bowing our heads, and said, "We will do whatever you ask. Give us the strength to always do your will."

He gave us the box of ointment and the bag of medicine and instructed us, "Return to the city of Habitation. Teach those who believe in my name to endure, just as I endured hardships for the sake of faith. I will reward you. Give to the poor whatever they need until I provide something greater, as I promised to give freely."

Peter asked, "Lord, you taught us to leave behind worldly possessions, and we have done so for your sake. How can we help the poor when we have nothing ourselves?"

The Lord replied, "Peter, you must understand the lesson I taught you. Don't you see that my name is more valuable than any treasure? The wisdom of God is worth more than gold, silver, or precious stones."

He handed them the bag of medicine and said, "Heal the sick in the city who believe in my name." Peter, hesitant to ask another question, signaled to John, who then asked, "Lord, we are afraid to speak too much, but you are asking us to heal. We have never learned how to be doctors. How can we heal as you ask?"

The Lord replied, "You are right, John. The doctors of this world heal the body, but the healers of souls heal the heart. First, heal their bodies with the power I give you, without using earthly medicine. Then they will believe in your ability to heal their hearts as well.

"As for the wealthy men in the city who ignored me and clung to their riches and pride, do not eat with them or become too close to them. Their influence could lead you into sin, just as it has led others away in the churches. Judge them wisely so that your ministry and my name may be honored in the churches."

The disciples agreed, saying, "Yes, this is right." They worshiped him again, and he helped them to their feet before departing in peace. Amen.

Irenaeus – Against Heresies (Selections)

Preface.

Some people have turned away from the truth and started spreading lies and confusing stories about family lines. As the apostle once said, these things only cause arguments instead of helping people grow in their faith. These tricky people use clever words to fool and trap those who don't know better. That's why, my friend, I felt I had to write this letter—to uncover and stop their tricks.

They twist God's words and mislead others, acting like they know more than the God who created everything. They claim to have secret knowledge and try to pull people away from the one true God, the Creator of heaven, earth, and all things. They use smooth talk to make their teachings sound good, but in truth, they teach dangerous and disrespectful ideas about God. They lead simple people to believe false things, and those people can't even tell the difference between truth and lies.

Lies never show up looking ugly, because then people would easily spot them. Instead, lies dress themselves up to look good—sometimes even better than the truth! Someone wiser than me once said, "A glass copy can look better than a real emerald to someone who doesn't know the difference." Or think about how hard it is for someone untrained to notice when brass is mixed with silver.

So I don't want anyone to be tricked and led away like sheep by wolves—especially when these false teachers pretend to be good and talk like us, even though what they believe is completely different. After reading some writings of Valentinus' followers and talking with a few of them myself, I decided it was important to explain their strange and dangerous ideas to you, my friend. These teachings are deep and confusing, and not everyone can understand them easily. But I want you to know them so you can warn others and help them stay away from this madness and disrespect toward Christ.

I'll do my best to clearly and briefly describe what these heretics—especially those who follow Ptolemaeus, a student of Valentinus—are saying. I'll also show how their teachings don't make sense and go against the truth. I'm not trained in fancy writing or public speaking. I'm just sharing this out of care and concern for you and your friends. These ideas have been hidden for a long time, but now, by God's kindness, they're being revealed—because, as Scripture says, "Nothing is hidden that won't be shown, and nothing is secret that won't be known."

Please don't expect me, living far away among the Celts and speaking a rough local language, to write with fancy words or elegant style—I've never learned that. Instead, I hope you'll accept my simple and honest writing. You're smarter than I am, so I trust you can take the small seeds I'm giving and help them grow. Share this truth with others in a way that they'll understand and believe.

I've worked hard to explain these teachings and to help you show why they're false. Now it's your turn, through the strength God gives you, to be a faithful teacher and guide to others. Help them stop being tricked by these smooth-sounding lies. Now I'll begin describing what these false teachers are spreading.

Chapter I

Strange Beliefs of Valentinus' Followers About the Origin, Names, and Pairs of Imaginary Aeons, and the

Bible Verses They Twist to Support Their Ideas

The followers of Valentinus say that far above everything, in a place no one can see or describe, there is a perfect being they call Proarche, Propator, or Bythus. They believe he is eternal, never created, and always peaceful. With him is a presence called Ennoea, also named Charis or Sige. Eventually, Bythus decided to create everything. He placed the beginning of creation into Sige, like a seed in a womb. She became pregnant and gave birth to Nous, who was like his father and could understand him fully. They also call Nous "Monogenes" (only-born), "Father," and "Beginning of All Things." With him came Aletheia. These four—Bythus, Sige, Nous, and Aletheia—form the first group, which they call the "root of all things."

Monogenes then created Logos (Word) and Zoe (Life). These two gave rise to Anthropos (Man) and Ecclesia (Church). Altogether, these eight beings are called the first "Ogdoad." Each one is seen as both male and female: Propator with Ennoea, Nous with Aletheia, Logos with Zoe, and Anthropos with Ecclesia.

These beings, called Aeons, were made to show the Father's greatness. To do this, they each created more beings. Logos and Zoe, after making Anthropos and Ecclesia, created ten more Aeons: Bythius and Mixis, Ageratos and Henosis, Autophyes and Hedone, Acinetos and Syncrasis, Monogenes and Macaria.

Then Anthropos and Ecclesia created twelve Aeons of their own, with names like Paracletus and Pistis, Patricos and Elpis, Metricos and Agape, Ainos and Synesis, Ecclesiasticus and Macariotes, Theletos and Sophia.

These are the thirty Aeons in their system, hidden in mystery and supposedly only known to certain teachers. They say this spiritual world, or Pleroma, has three parts: eight Aeons (Ogdoad), ten Aeons

(Decad), and twelve Aeons (Duodecad). That's why they claim Jesus didn't do anything publicly until he was thirty years old—because it matches the number of Aeons.

They even try to prove this idea with the Bible story of the workers in the vineyard, where some are hired at the 1st, 3rd, 6th, 9th, and 11th hours. When you add those hours together, they say, you get thirty—and that's their big mystery. They use verses like this, pulling them out of context, to make their strange ideas sound like they come from Scripture.

Chapter II

The First Father Was Known Only to Monogenes; Sophia's Mistake, Her Shapeless Child, and Her Rescue by Horos; The Creation of Christ and the Spirit to Complete the Aeons; How Jesus Was Made

They say that the First Father, called the Propator, could only be known by Monogenes—also called Nous—who came directly from him. The other spiritual beings, called Aeons, couldn't see or understand the Father at all. Only Nous fully enjoyed thinking about the Father's endless greatness and wanted to share this with the other Aeons. But the Father, through a being named Sige (which means "Silence"), held him back. The goal was to let the others grow curious about the Father on their own.

The other Aeons quietly wished to see the source of their life. But one of them acted too fast. This was Sophia, the youngest of the twelve Aeons that came from Anthropos and Ecclesia. She tried to reach the Father without her partner Theletos. Her desire came from wanting to know the Father, but she wasn't ready—unlike Nous, who had a close connection with Him. Sophia's longing became too strong and painful, and she nearly lost herself in her obsession. She could have disappeared into the Father's greatness if not for a powerful being named Horos, who stopped her. He helped her return to herself and realize that the Father could never be fully understood.

Others tell the story differently. They say Sophia tried something impossible and ended up creating a formless, imperfect being—something only her female nature could produce. When she saw what she had made, she felt sad and afraid it might ruin her. She panicked and didn't know how to hide her mistake. Eventually, she changed her mind and tried to return to the Father, but she was too weak. So she asked for help. The other Aeons, especially Nous, also prayed for her. This is how they say physical matter came to be—from ignorance, fear, sadness, and confusion.

Later, the Father created Horos through Monogenes, without needing a partner. Horos had both male and female traits. They also gave him other names like Stauros and Lytrotes. Horos cleaned and stabilized Sophia, returning her to her rightful place. Her inner thought and emotion, called "enthymesis," were taken out of her and placed outside the spiritual world. Though this enthymesis was somewhat like an Aeon, it had no form or strength. That's why they say it was weak and feminine.

Once this being was moved out, and Sophia was back in her proper place, Monogenes and the Father created a new pair—Christ and the Holy Spirit. This was to protect the Aeons from making the same mistake Sophia did and to complete the full number of Aeons. Christ taught the Aeons how to be in harmony with their partners. He explained that only Monogenes could truly know the Father, who cannot be seen or fully understood. The Aeons live forever because of the hidden part of the Father, and they were created through the part that could be understood—that is, through the Son.

The Holy Spirit helped the Aeons feel grateful and at peace. After this, they say all the Aeons became equal, like Nous, Logos, Anthropos, and Christ. The female Aeons became like Aletheia, Zoe, Spiritus, and Ecclesia. Everything was balanced and calm, and the Aeons praised the First Father joyfully.

Out of thankfulness, the Aeons all offered their best qualities. They blended these together to create someone beautiful and perfect—Jesus, the brightest being in the spiritual world. They called him Savior, Christ, Logos, and Everything, because he was made from the best parts of all the Aeons. Along with him, angels were created to stay by his side and serve him.

Chapter III

Bible Verses These Heretics Use to Support Their Beliefs

This is what they say happened in the spiritual realm: Sophia, one of the Aeons, almost disappeared into the full divine essence because of her desire to understand the Father. But she was saved and stabilized by a being named Horos, also called Stauros, Lytrotes, Carpistes, Horothetes, and Metagoges. After she repented, the Father created Christ and the Holy Spirit. Then later, another Christ, also called the Savior, was created from the shared gifts of the Aeons. They claim this special knowledge wasn't given to everyone—only to those who could understand it—and that Jesus revealed it through parables.

They say Jesus' thirty years of public silence represent the thirty Aeons, as does the parable of the workers in the vineyard. According to them, Paul also talks about these Aeons when he says "to all the generations of the Aeons of the Aeon." They even claim we acknowledge these Aeons ourselves when we say phrases like "forever and ever." They apply every mention of "Aeon" in Scripture to support this belief.

They also say that the twelve Aeons are symbolized by Jesus being twelve years old when He spoke with the teachers, and by His choosing twelve apostles. The remaining eighteen Aeons, they say, are shown by Jesus spending eighteen months with His disciples after His resurrection. They find even more meaning in the letters of Jesus' name—saying the first two letters, Iota and Eta, stand for ten and eight, which total eighteen. They claim that's why Jesus said, "Not one iota or one stroke of the law will pass away," using that letter as a symbol of the Aeons.

They believe the suffering of the twelfth Aeon is shown by Judas, the twelfth apostle, betraying Jesus—and by Jesus suffering in the twelfth month, since they think He only preached for a year after being baptized. They also point to the woman who had been bleeding for twelve years. When she touched Jesus' robe and was healed, they say it symbolized the suffering Aeon, who was reaching out endlessly but was healed when she came in contact with truth—represented by the hem of His robe, which stands for Aletheia, the first of four Aeons. The power that healed her, they say, was Horos, who separated her pain from her.

They claim the Savior came from all the Aeons and contains everything in Himself. To prove it, they quote "Every male that opens the womb," saying Jesus "opened the womb" of Sophia's inner thoughts when they were cast out of the spiritual world. This, they say, is the second group of eight Aeons. They also use Paul's words, like

"He is all things," and "All things are in Him," and "The fullness of God lives in Him," to support this idea.

They also teach that Horos has two powers: one to hold things together and one to divide them. As the one who supports, he's called Stauros; as the one who separates, he's Horos. They say Jesus pointed to this when He said, "Whoever doesn't carry their cross can't follow me," and, "Take up your cross and follow me." That's the support side. But when He said, "I didn't come to bring peace, but a sword," that shows the dividing side.

They claim John described Horos too, when he said Jesus has a fan in His hand to separate wheat from chaff. The fan, they say, is the cross, which destroys bad things like fire burns chaff but saves the good, like wheat being cleaned. Paul, they argue, also pointed to this when he said, "The message of the cross is foolishness to those who are dying, but to us who are being saved it is the power of God," and, "I only boast in the cross of Christ."

This, they say, is their version of how the universe and the spiritual world were made. But they twist Scripture to fit their made-up stories—not just the gospels and letters, but also the law and the prophets. Because these writings have symbolic and deep meanings, people who don't stay strong in their faith in one true God and in Jesus Christ can be misled by these false teachings.

Chapter IV

What the Heretics Say About Achamoth and How the Visible World Was Created from Her Emotions

Here's what they claim happened outside the spiritual world (Pleroma): Sophia, also known as Achamoth, was pushed out of the divine realm along with her emotional suffering. In the darkness where she ended up, she had no shape or form—like a child born too early—because she didn't receive anything from a male partner. But Christ, who was still in the higher spiritual world, felt sorry for her. He stretched himself beyond a boundary called Stauros to give her a basic shape—just her physical form, not her mind. Then he pulled back and left her alone. The idea was that being separated from the spiritual world would help her long for something better. Christ and the Holy Spirit left behind a kind of "scent" of eternal life in her.

Because of this, people call her by two names: "Sophia," because she came from the original Sophia, and "Holy Spirit," because of the Spirit who was with Christ. After getting a body and some awareness, Achamoth realized Christ was gone and tried to find him. But she was stopped by Horos. They say Horos shouted the word "Iao," and that's where the name comes from. Since she couldn't pass Horos, and because she was alone and full of emotional turmoil, she started feeling many things—sadness because she couldn't reach the light, fear that she might stop existing, and deep confusion. These emotions came from ignorance—not ignorance like her "mother" Sophia had, which was from a mistake, but from being naturally unable to understand things. Then she developed another emotion: a deep desire to return to the one who gave her life.

The heretics say that all these emotions turned into the building blocks of the world. Her desire to go back to the light became the souls of all people, including the soul of the creator god (whom they call the Demiurge). Her fear and sadness became everything else in the world. For example, her tears turned into seas, rivers, and all liquids; her joy created light; and her sadness and confusion made physical matter. At one moment she would cry over being alone in darkness, then laugh thinking about the light, then feel scared again, then get confused all over again.

So what does this all lead to? According to them, this complicated story explains how everything in the world came to be. Each teacher adds their own twist, saying different emotions caused different parts of the world. They don't share these ideas openly—they only tell people who are willing to pay and go through effort to learn these "deep secrets." But this is very different from what Jesus said: "You received freely, so give freely." Their version is overly mysterious and hard to understand—and it seems made up for those who want something dramatic and false. Who wouldn't spend everything they had to learn that the oceans came from someone's tears, light came from a smile, and physical matter came from her panic?

Let me help by offering a small idea based on their thinking. We know that some water in the world is fresh—like rain, rivers, and springs—while other water is salty—like the sea. But if all of it came from Achamoth's tears, wouldn't it all be salty? So maybe just the saltwater came from tears, and the freshwater came from her sweat when she was upset. Since tears all taste the same, it's hard to believe they made both fresh and salty water. So it's more likely some came from her tears, and some from sweat. But as for the hot or acidic waters in the world, I guess we're just supposed to guess where they came from. This is what their theory leads to.

They continue by saying that after suffering so much, Achamoth finally cried out to the light that had left her—Christ. But instead of coming down himself, Christ sent the Paraclete, the Savior. The Father gave this Savior full power and authority, and so did the other Aeons. They say that through him, everything was made—both visible and invisible, like thrones and powers. He came down with angels. At first, Achamoth was shy and hid her face, but after seeing his greatness, she got stronger and ran to meet him. He gave her intelligence and helped her recover from her emotional pain. But he didn't erase her emotions completely, because they had already taken root and couldn't be destroyed.

Instead, he separated her emotions from her, mixed them together, and turned them into raw material. This way, two types of things were formed: one made of negative emotions and the other made from her desire to return to the light, which could still feel pain. This transformation of emotional energy into matter is why, they say, the Savior basically created the world. After being freed from her pain, Achamoth looked in wonder at the angels around the Savior. In her amazement, she gave birth to new beings—some looked like her, and some were spiritual beings like the angels.

Chapter V

The Making of the Demiurge and His Role in Creating the World Outside the Divine Realm

According to their story, there are three kinds of beings. First, there's matter, which came from emotional suffering. Second, there's the "animal" type, which came from a turn toward the light. Third, there's the spiritual type, which Achamoth herself gave birth to. She tried to shape all three kinds, but couldn't form the spiritual one because it was too much like her. So she focused on shaping the animal type and tried to share the teachings of the Savior through it.

They say that from this animal nature, she created a being who became the father and ruler of everything that came afterward. He ruled over both animal-like beings (which they called "right-handed") and material beings (called "left-handed"), both of which he made—though not by himself, but secretly guided by his mother. Because of this, they gave him many names: Metropator (Mother-Father), Apator (without a father), Demiurge (Creator), and Father. He is said to be the father of animal beings and the creator of material ones—ruling over everything.

They also say that the Savior used Achamoth to create copies, or "images," of the spiritual beings called Aeons. Achamoth stayed hidden from the Demiurge, but she looked like the invisible Father. The Demiurge looked like the only Son, and the angels and archangels he created resembled the other Aeons.

They claim this Demiurge became the god and father of everything outside the spiritual world. He made both animal and material things. He separated different types of matter, gave form to shapeless things, created both heaven and earth, and became the builder of everything physical and animal, light and heavy, rising and falling. He also made seven heavens and lives just above them. Because of this, they call him "Hebdomas" (the one over seven), and they call his mother Achamoth "Ogdoad" (the one over eight), keeping the idea of the original eight-part system of the spiritual world.

They say the seven heavens are actually intelligent beings, or angels. The Demiurge is also considered an angel who looks like God. They even say that Paradise is a fourth powerful angel, living above the third heaven. This angel supposedly gave Adam some qualities during a conversation.

They believe the Demiurge thought he made everything by himself, but he actually worked with the creative power of his mother, Achamoth. He built the heavens but didn't understand them. He made people but didn't truly know them. He formed the earth without realizing what it was. He didn't even know his own mother existed and believed he was the only god. Achamoth purposely made him think this way so he would become the leader of his own world and act as ruler over all creation.

They give Achamoth many names: Ogdoad, Sophia, Earth, Jerusalem, Holy Spirit, and sometimes even "Lord." She lives in a place above the Demiurge but below the spiritual world.

All material things, they say, came from three emotions: fear, sadness, and confusion. Animal beings came from fear and turning toward the light. The Demiurge came from this turn, too. All other animals—like wild beasts and even humans—came from fear. Because of this, the Demiurge can't understand spiritual beings. He thinks he's the only god and says through prophets, "I am God, and there is no one else."

They say evil spirits came from sadness—this includes the devil (whom they call Cosmocrator), demons, bad angels, and all other wicked spirits. The Demiurge is the son of Achamoth, and Cosmocrator was created by the Demiurge. The devil knows what's above him because he's a spirit, but the Demiurge is only animal and doesn't. Achamoth lives above the heavens, the Demiurge in the heavens (the seven heavens), and the devil lives in our world.

The elements of the world came from confusion. The earth came from her mental numbness, water from her fearful trembling, air from her grief, and fire—which causes death and decay—was hidden in all of these. They say even ignorance was mixed in with these three emotions.

After making the world, the Demiurge created the physical part of humans. He didn't form them from dry ground, but from a hidden, liquid-like substance. Then, as they explain it, he breathed life into them—this breath was the animal part of humans. This part resembled God in image but was not made of the same substance. The animal soul was more like God in likeness and was called "spirit of life" because it came from something spiritual. Finally, the human body was wrapped in skin, which represents our outer flesh.

But they also claim that the Demiurge didn't know that his mother, Achamoth, had secretly added a spiritual part to the humans he made. She did this by reflecting on the angels who served the Savior and creating something spiritual, just like herself. Without the Demiurge knowing, she placed this spiritual seed inside the animal soul. So even though the Demiurge thought he was just making an ordinary man, Achamoth had made him spiritual too. Over time, this spiritual part would grow stronger inside the human body and become ready to understand truth.

So, according to their belief, the man the Demiurge created was unknowingly made spiritual by Sophia's action. He had an animal soul from the Demiurge, a physical body from the earth, a flesh covering from matter, and a spiritual soul from Achamoth. They call this spiritual part "Ecclesia," a symbol of the true spiritual community above.

Chapter VI

The Three Types of People According to These Heretics: Why They Say Good Deeds Don't Matter for Them but Do for Others, and How Their Morals Have Gone Bad

These heretics say there are three kinds of things: material, animal, and spiritual. They claim that anything made of matter (which they call "on the left side") is doomed to die because it can't be made eternal. Things that are "animal" (which they call "on the right side") are in-between—they can go toward the material or the spiritual, depending on which way they lean. Spiritual things, they say, were sent here to mix with animal beings so they could take on form and learn through experience. They say this is what "the salt" and "the light of the world" really mean. The animal part, they believe, needed to be trained through the senses. That's why, according to them, the world was made and why the Savior came—to help the animal nature, which has free will, find salvation.

They also teach that Jesus took something spiritual from Achamoth (a being they believe in), was given an animal body by the creator of the world, and wore a special body that was perfectly designed so it could be seen and touched and suffer pain. Still, they insist He didn't take on any material substance because matter, they say, can't be saved. They believe that in the end, everything will be complete once all the spiritual people gain full knowledge of God. This knowledge, called Gnosis, makes them perfect. They believe they are these spiritual people.

As for "animal" people, they say these folks are taught in basic ways—by doing good things and by faith alone, without full knowledge. They say that people in the Church, like us, are these animal types. That's why, they argue, we need to do good works in order to be saved. But for themselves, they claim they'll definitely be saved—not because of what they do, but because they were born spiritual. Just like matter can't be saved, they say that spiritual people can't be corrupted, no matter what they do. They compare themselves to gold covered in filth: the dirt doesn't ruin the gold underneath, so their spiritual nature stays untouched even if their actions are bad.

Because of this belief, the "most perfect" among them live without any shame, doing things the Bible clearly says will keep people out of God's kingdom. They have no problem eating meat that's been offered to idols, claiming it doesn't hurt them. They're even the first to show up at pagan celebrations and wild events. Some of them even go to the violent gladiator shows where people fight animals or each other—something both God and people find disgusting. Others give in to all kinds of sexual desires and say that physical pleasures should be allowed for the body, while spiritual things belong to the soul.

Some of them use these teachings to take advantage of women they've misled, and the women later confess this when they return to the Church. Others go even further—falling in love with married women, breaking up families, and marrying the women themselves. Some pretend at first to live purely with women as if they're sisters, but later it's revealed that the woman became pregnant by the so-called "brother."

They do many more disgusting and offensive things, but still look down on people like us—those who try not to sin, even in thought or speech—calling us ignorant and weak. At the same time, they brag about being perfect and God's chosen ones. They say that we were only given grace for a while, and it will be taken away again. But they believe they own grace permanently because it came down to them in a mysterious and special way, and they say this means they deserve to receive even more. So they claim it's their duty to always practice what they call the "mystery of union."

To convince people to believe them, they even say things like, "Anyone who doesn't love a woman enough to have her isn't living in the truth and won't find it. But if a person does sleep with a woman just because they have strong desires, then they also won't find the truth." That's why they say we "animal" people—people of the world—must live pure lives and do good works so we can at least reach a middle place. But for them, who call themselves "spiritual and perfect," they claim that none of this is necessary. They say it's not about how you act, but about a seed that came from a higher place and is now growing to its full form here on Earth.

Chapter VII

What Happens to Achamoth and Different Types of People When Everything Is Complete; Their False Beliefs About Christ's Birth, the Prophets, and the Creator

These heretics believe that when all the spiritual seeds have become perfect, their mother Achamoth will leave the middle place and enter the Pleroma, the place of divine fullness. There, she will be united with the Savior, who comes from all the Aeons, as her husband. Together they will form a spiritual marriage, and the Pleroma will be their wedding place. They say the spiritual seeds—once separated from their animal souls and turned into pure spirits—will secretly and irresistibly enter the Pleroma too. These spirits will become the brides of angels who serve the Savior. The Demiurge, the lower creator god, will move into the middle place, which they say is also the place of his mother Sophia. In that same middle place, the souls of good people will find rest. But no animal nature will be allowed into the Pleroma. When all this is finished, they say a hidden fire will burst out, destroy all matter, and then burn itself out forever. They claim that the Demiurge didn't know any of this until the Savior arrived.

Some of them also teach that the Demiurge created Christ as his own son, but with an animal nature. They say the prophets talked about this Christ. According to them, He passed through Mary like water through a pipe and didn't take anything from her. When He was baptized, a dove from the Pleroma came down on Him—that dove was the true Savior, made by the Aeons. They also believe this Savior had inside Him the spiritual seed from Achamoth. So they say Jesus was made of four parts: a spiritual part from Achamoth, an animal body from the Demiurge, a divine part from the Savior (the dove), and a special form made with perfect skill. They insist that the real Christ never suffered, because He couldn't suffer—He was beyond human pain and could not be seen or harmed. They even say that the spirit of Christ left Jesus before He faced Pilate, so He wouldn't feel pain. They argue that even the seed from Achamoth inside Him didn't suffer, since it was spiritual and couldn't be touched—even by the Demiurge. Only the animal body, they say, went through pain, and that was done just to give a symbol of the higher Christ—the one who stretched Himself across the Cross and gave Achamoth her shape. They claim all of this mirrors what happened above in the spiritual world.

They also say that souls containing Achamoth's seed are better than all other souls. The Demiurge loves them more, even though he doesn't know why—he thinks they are special because of his own favor. That's why, they say, he gave them to prophets, priests, and kings. They claim that many of the things spoken by the prophets came from this seed, since it had a very high and divine nature. They say the mother (Achamoth) also spoke through the Demiurge and through the souls he made. They divide the prophecies into three groups: some were spoken by Achamoth, some by her seed, and some by the Demiurge. In the same way, they say Jesus spoke some things inspired by the Savior, some by the mother, and others by the Demiurge. This, they say, will be explained more later.

The Demiurge didn't understand the higher things above him. Even when the prophets spoke, he misunderstood their messages. Sometimes he thought they came from a spiritual power that could stir itself up. Other times, he thought the messages came from human thinking, or from clever people who tricked others. So he stayed ignorant until Jesus came. They say that when the Savior arrived, He taught the Demiurge everything. The Demiurge was happy to learn and gave his full support to Jesus. They believe the Demiurge is the centurion in the Gospel who said, "I also am a man under authority, with soldiers under me. When I tell them what to do, they do it." They also claim that the Demiurge will keep running the world for now, as long as it's needed. He'll take special care of the Church, because he knows that a reward is waiting for him: the chance to live with his mother in the middle place.

They believe there are three kinds of people: material, animal, and spiritual. These types are represented by Cain, Abel, and Seth. They say these three kinds don't exist together in one person anymore—they are now completely separate types of people. Material people, they say, are doomed to die and disappear. Animal people can either choose good and rest in the middle place or choose evil and also be destroyed. But the spiritual people, who came from Achamoth, have been growing and being trained in righteous souls from long ago until now. At first, they were weak when Achamoth sent them out, but once they become fully developed, they will be given as brides to the Savior's angels. Meanwhile, their animal souls will stay forever with the Demiurge in the middle place. They even divide animal souls further, saying some are naturally good and able to receive the spiritual seed, while others are naturally evil and never able to receive it at all.

Chapter VIII

How the Valentinians Twist the Scriptures to Fit Their Own Ideas

This is the system the Valentinians believe in—a system not taught by the prophets, not delivered by Jesus, and not passed down by the apostles. Still, they claim they have a better understanding than anyone else. They don't build their beliefs on Scripture. Instead, they take ideas from other places and try to make them sound like they come from the Bible. They mix the sayings of Jesus, the prophets, and the apostles with their own strange ideas so it seems like the Scriptures support them. But in doing so, they rip verses out of context, rearrange them, and twist their meaning. It's like taking a beautiful statue of a king, made from expensive jewels, pulling it apart, and using the same jewels to build a sloppy figure of a dog or a fox. Then they say, "Look, this is the same statue the artist made." The parts are the same, but the form is completely wrong. In the same way, they take God's Word and bend it to support their false stories. We've already talked about how far they go with this when it comes to their ideas about the Pleroma.

Now, for things outside the Pleroma, they try to match their ideas to Scripture in strange ways. For example, they say Jesus came near the end of time and suffered to show what happened to the last Aeon. His death, they say, marked the end of the trouble among the Aeons. When Jesus raised the synagogue ruler's 12-year-old daughter, they claim this girl stood for Achamoth. They say Christ stretched Himself to shape her and bring her back to the light she had lost. When Paul said, "Last of all, He appeared to me as to one born out of due time," they say he was talking about Achamoth, because she existed outside the Pleroma. They also claim that when Paul said a woman should wear a veil because of the angels, he was talking about Achamoth putting on a veil when the Savior came to her. Moses covering his face with a veil is said to show the same thing.

They say Jesus' suffering on the cross mirrors the emotional pain of Sophia (Achamoth). When He cried out, "My God, why have You forsaken Me?" they say He was showing how she felt abandoned. His sorrow ("My soul is very sorrowful") shows her grief. His fear ("Let this cup pass from Me") reveals her anxiety. His confusion ("What shall I say?") represents her being lost and unsure.

They claim Jesus also revealed the three types of people. The material person is shown when someone asks to follow Him and Jesus replies, "The Son of Man has no place to rest." The animal type is shown in the one who wants to follow but asks to say goodbye to his family first. Jesus responds, "No one who looks back is fit for God's kingdom." They say this man, like others attached to wealth or unsure about following Jesus, is animal in nature. The spiritual type is shown when Jesus says, "Let the dead bury their own dead, but you go and preach the kingdom," or when He tells Zacchaeus, "Come down quickly; today I must stay at your house." These, they say, were truly spiritual.

They also interpret the parable of the woman who mixes yeast into three measures of flour. According to them, the woman is Sophia, the flour is the three types of people—material, animal, and spiritual—and the yeast is the Savior. Paul, too, is said to support this. They point to verses where he says, "Those who are earthy are like the earth," "The animal man doesn't receive the Spirit," and "The spiritual person judges all things." They claim Paul was talking about the Demiurge as the "animal man" who didn't know his spiritual mother, her children, or the Aeons in the Pleroma.

They also say that when Paul talked about "first-fruits" being holy, and so the "whole lump" is holy too, he meant that the first-fruits are the spiritual people and the lump is the animal Church. They claim the Savior mixed the lump with Himself just like yeast mixes with dough.

They believe Achamoth, who wandered outside the Pleroma, was shaped by Christ and searched for by the Savior. They say this is what Jesus meant when He spoke of finding the one lost sheep. That sheep, they claim, is their mother, who gave birth to the Church and lived outside the Pleroma, experiencing emotional suffering. From her pain, they say, matter came into being. The woman who swept the house and found her lost coin is said to be the higher Sophia, who lost her desire (or thought) and found it again when everything was purified by the Savior's coming. This, they say, restored her to the Pleroma.

Simeon, who held baby Jesus and thanked God before dying, is said to represent the Demiurge. When the Savior arrived, the Demiurge realized his new place and gave thanks to the First Father (Bythus). Anna, the prophetess who lived with her husband for seven years and stayed a widow until she saw Jesus, stands for Achamoth. They say she waited in the middle place for the Savior to come back and take her to her rightful partner. Jesus spoke of her, they claim, when He said, "Wisdom is shown to be right by her children." Paul also said, "We speak wisdom among the mature," which they say refers to her. They even believe Paul spoke about the spiritual pairings in the Pleroma when he talked about marriage and said, "This is a great mystery, but I speak about Christ and the Church."

They also teach that John, the disciple of Jesus, talked about the first group of eight beings (the Ogdoad). They say John started his Gospel to explain how everything began. He spoke of the first being God created—His only Son—who held the seeds of everything. Through Him came the Word, and the Word shaped all the Aeons. That's why John began his Gospel by saying: "In the beginning was the Word, and the Word was with God, and the Word was God." He shows that God, the Beginning, and the Word are united and created everything. "The Beginning" is from the Father. The Word is from the Beginning. So, "In the beginning was the Word" means the Word was in the Son. "The Word was with God" means He was from the

Beginning. "The Word was God" means the Son is divine. Then, "He was with God in the beginning" shows how He was made.

"All things were made by Him"—the Word gave shape to everything. "In Him was life"—which, they say, means deep union. "The life was the light of men"—this light, they say, is the being called Zoe (Life), who gave form to Anthropos (Humanity) and Ecclesia (the Church). Zoe enlightened them, so she's their light. Paul also said, "Whatever makes something visible is light," so Zoe is their light. This is how John supposedly revealed the second group of four beings: the Word and Zoe, Anthropos and Ecclesia. And he also revealed the first group of four: the Father, Grace (Charis), the Only-Begotten (Monogenes), and Truth (Aletheia).

According to them, John described all eight: the Father, Grace, the Only-Begotten, Truth, the Word, Zoe, Humanity, and the Church. These are the teachings of Ptolemaeus.

Chapter IX

Answering the False Interpretations of These Heretics

You can now see, my friend, how these people fool themselves and misuse the Scriptures to support their strange beliefs. That's why I've shown you the way they talk—so you can recognize how sneaky and wrong they really are. If John had wanted to teach about their supposed group of eight divine beings (the Ogdoad), he would have listed them in the right order. He would have started with the first four, which they say are the most important, then added the next four, so that the full list would make sense. But instead, they claim that after a long break, as if John forgot and suddenly remembered, he mentioned the first four at the end.

Also, if John meant to describe spiritual pairings (like husband and wife), he wouldn't have left out names like Ecclesia (the Church). If he had listed the male figures, we should expect the female ones too. Or, if he had included the wives of others, he would have told us the wife of Anthropos as well, instead of leaving us to guess who she was.

This clearly shows how wrong their explanation is. When John wrote about the one true God, the Almighty, and about Jesus Christ, God's only Son through whom everything was made, he said that this Jesus is the Son of God, the true light who gives light to everyone, the Creator of the world, and the one who came to His own people and became human. But these heretics twist John's words and say there's a different "Only-Begotten," whom they call Arche. They also say there's another Savior, another Word (Logos), and another Christ who came to fix the Pleroma. They steal each name and idea from Scripture and twist them to support their own made-up system. In their version, John isn't talking about Jesus at all. If he mentions the Father, Grace (Charis), the Only-Begotten (Monogenes), Truth (Aletheia), the Word, Life (Zoe), Humanity (Anthropos), and the Church (Ecclesia), then they say he's just describing their imaginary Ogdoad. But in that case, there's no Jesus and no Christ—the one John actually followed.

It's clear that John was not describing their made-up divine pairings, but was speaking about our Lord Jesus Christ. John himself proves it when he writes, "The Word became flesh and lived among us." But in the Valentinians' view, the true Word never became flesh. They say it was the "Savior" who took on a body made from a special mix of all the Aeons, and that this happened later than the creation of the Word.

You need to understand, then, that Jesus—the one who lived among us and suffered for us—is the same as the Word of God. If some other divine being had taken on a body to save us, then maybe John would've been talking about someone else. But the truth is, the

Son of the one true God, the Only-Begotten, came down by God's will and became flesh to save us. So John isn't talking about anyone else or some group of Aeons. He's talking about Jesus Christ.

The Valentinians say that the Savior took on an animal body—one formed with great care to be able to suffer—but this is not what the Bible teaches. Real flesh is what God gave to Adam when He made him from the dust. And John says it was this kind of real flesh that the Word became. So, their theory about a first-born group of eight divine beings falls apart. All those names—Word, Only-Begotten, Life, Light, Savior, Christ, Son of God, and the One who became flesh for us—are talking about the same person: Jesus. If that's true, then their Ogdoad and the whole system built around it completely collapses.

They also collect words and phrases from all over Scripture and twist them out of their original meaning. It's like when people take random lines from Homer's poems to make it look like Homer wrote about something he never actually wrote about. A person who doesn't know Homer might fall for it, but someone who's read the poems would recognize the lines—even if they know the story being told isn't really from Homer.

For example, someone might try to say Homer wrote a story about Hercules being sent by Eurystheus to the underworld to get the guard dog there, and then use real Homeric lines pulled from stories about Ulysses, Priam, Menelaus, and others to make it look convincing. If you didn't know better, the story might seem real. But once you place each quote back in its original story, the fake tale falls apart. In the same way, if someone truly holds to the truth they received when they were baptized, they'll recognize the words of Scripture, but not the twisted meanings the heretics give them. They'll know the "gems" are real, but they won't mistake the ugly, made-up fox statue for the true image of the King. Once you put all the verses back in their right place, you can clearly see that the heretics' teachings have no real foundation.

To wrap this up properly, it helps to point out one more thing: even the leaders of this false teaching don't agree with each other. They each seem to be following different lies, as if led by different spirits of confusion. This alone proves that the Church's message is strong and unchanging, while the ideas of these heretics are just a mess of made-up stories and contradictions.

Chapter X

The Unified Faith of the Church Around the World

The Church, even though it is spread all over the world, from one end of the earth to the other, has received the same faith from the apostles and their followers. This faith teaches that there is one God, the all-powerful Father, who created heaven, earth, the sea, and everything in them. It also teaches belief in one Lord, Jesus Christ, the Son of God, who became human to save us. And it teaches belief in the Holy Spirit, who spoke through the prophets about God's plans—about the coming of Christ, His birth from a virgin, His suffering, His rising from the dead, His return to heaven in a physical body, and His future return from heaven in the glory of the Father. When He returns, He will gather all things together, raise all people from the dead, and judge everyone with justice. Those who are evil—including fallen angels, demons, and ungodly people—will be sent into eternal fire. But those who are good—who are righteous, holy, and have kept God's commandments and remained in His love, whether from the beginning of their Christian life or after turning back to God—will be given eternal life and surrounded by everlasting glory.

As I already mentioned, the Church holds firmly to this faith and message. Even though its members live in many parts of the world, it is as if they all live in the same house. The Church believes with one heart and soul, teaches the same truths, and passes them on as if it had one voice. Even though people speak different languages, the meaning of the message is always the same. The churches in Germany, Spain, Gaul (France), the East, Egypt, Libya, and in the central parts of the world all believe and teach the same things. Just like the sun shines the same light across the whole world, the truth of the Gospel shines everywhere for anyone who wants to know it.

No church leader, no matter how smart or skilled in speaking, can teach anything different than this faith—because no one is greater than the one true Teacher, Jesus. On the other hand, someone who isn't a great speaker doesn't weaken or damage the faith either. The truth is always the same. A person who explains it in detail doesn't add anything new, and someone who explains only the basics doesn't take anything away.

Just because people have different levels of understanding doesn't mean they can change what the faith teaches. That doesn't mean we should invent another god, as if the one who created and keeps the world going isn't enough. We shouldn't invent another Christ or another Son of God. People with deeper understanding simply help us better explain what God has already revealed. They help us see how the parables and teachings fit together with the bigger picture of salvation. They help us understand why God has been patient with fallen angels and disobedient people. They explain why God made some things temporary and others eternal, some heavenly and others earthly. They show how God, though invisible, appeared differently to different prophets. They teach us why God made several covenants with people and what each one means. They help us understand what

Paul meant when he said, "God shut everyone up in unbelief so He could show mercy to all."

They explain why God's Word became human and suffered for us, and why the Son of God came at the end of time rather than at the beginning. They explore what Scripture says about the end of the world and the future, and they teach how God brought Gentiles—who once had no hope—into His family along with the saints. They help us understand how our weak, mortal bodies will be changed into immortal, incorruptible ones. They also explain verses like, "That is a people who was not a people" and "She is loved who was not loved," and "More are the children of the deserted woman than of her who had a husband." Paul himself, when talking about things like this, said, "Oh, the depth of the riches of the wisdom and knowledge of God! How impossible it is to understand His decisions and ways!"

Real wisdom is not about dreaming up a flawed Aeon who supposedly created the world, or a female figure who gave birth to him. It's not about inventing some imaginary world filled with thirty or even countless Aeons, as some false teachers claim. True wisdom is found in the one faith held by the Catholic Church across the whole world, a faith that has never changed—as we've already said.

Chapter XI

The Teachings of Valentinus and His Followers

Let's now take a look at how these heretics, even though they talk about the same ideas and use the same names, can't agree with each other. Their views are often inconsistent and confusing. First, there's Valentinus, who shaped the older Gnostic ideas into his own version. He said there was a pair of beings, a Dyad, who can't be fully described. One he called "Unspeakable" and the other "Silence." From this Dyad came another pair: one called the "Father" and the other "Truth." These four made up the first group. Then, from them came Word (Logos) and Life (Zoe), and also Man (Anthropos) and Church (Ecclesia). This gave them the first group of eight spiritual beings—the Ogdoad.

Valentinus said that Word and Life produced ten other powers, and Man and Church produced twelve. One of the twelve separated from the rest and caused the creation of the universe. He also claimed there were two beings called Horos. One stood between the perfect spiritual realm (Pleroma) and the unknowable Father, acting like a border. The other separated their mother figure from the Pleroma. Christ, he said, wasn't created by the beings inside the Pleroma, but by the mother who had been cast out. She made Him out of her memory of better things—but also with a shadow. Christ, being male, separated from the shadow and returned to the Pleroma. But the mother stayed with the shadow and, having lost her spiritual part, gave birth to another son—the Demiurge. Valentinus called this Demiurge the ruler of everything beneath him.

He also said that with the Demiurge came a left-hand power, similar to what some other Gnostics believed. Sometimes he claimed that Jesus came from Theletus, a being separated from the mother but joined to the others. Other times, he said Jesus came from Christ, who returned to the Pleroma. And at other times still, he said Jesus came from Man and Church. He also said the Holy Spirit came from Truth (Aletheia), to help the Aeons grow spiritually by secretly entering them. This way, the Aeons would produce the "plants of truth."

Then there was Secundus, who said the first group of eight consisted of two sets of four: one representing light and the other darkness. He taught that the power which fell away didn't come directly from the thirty Aeons, but from what they had produced.

Another teacher among them wanted to sound even more spiritual, so he made up a new version of the first four beings. He said that before anything else existed, there was a being called Proarche—above all thought, speech, and names. He called it "Unity" (Monotes). Along with Unity was another power he called "Oneness" (Henotes). These two didn't create anything outside themselves, but together they produced the first being, called the Monad. With the Monad came another power he called Hen (One). These four—Unity, Oneness, Monad, and One—were the start of everything else.

Wow—what nonsense! It's hard not to laugh at the boldness of someone who made up such ridiculous names without shame. Just listen to it: Proarche and Monotes, Henotes and Monad. It's obvious he just invented them all himself. No one before him had ever said these things. So, if he hadn't shown up, apparently the truth would still be nameless! But if people are allowed to make up whatever names they want, then why not use ones that people actually know? We could say there's a Proarche who stretches across everything, and along with it there's a power we'll call "Gourd." With the Gourd is another power called "Utter Emptiness." Together they produce something tasty and visible—the "Cucumber." And with the Cucumber is another power, the "Melon." These—Gourd, Emptiness, Cucumber, and Melon—give rise to all the other foolish "fruits" of Valentinus' thinking.

If it's okay to take the language we use to talk about the universe and force it onto made-up spiritual beings, then what's stopping us from making up our own names that make more sense and are easier to understand?

Some others came up with different names for their first group of eight beings. They called them Proarche, Anennoetos (Unthinkable), Arrhetos (Unspeakable), and Aoratos (Invisible). From Proarche came Arche; from Anennoetos came Acataleptos (Unknowable); from

Arrhetos came Anonomastos (Nameless); and from Aoratos came Agennetos (Unbegotten). This, they said, was their complete Ogdoad. They claimed these powers came before even Bythus and Silence, to make their beings sound more perfect and smarter than anyone else's.

To people who say things like this, we can rightly say: "You're just playing with words!" Even about Bythus, they can't agree. Some say he has no partner and is neither male nor female, or maybe not even anything at all. Others say he's both male and female, like a hermaphrodite. Still others say he has Silence (Sige) as a partner to form the first spiritual union.

What a mess of conflicting ideas—all pretending to be divine wisdom.

Chapter XII

The Teachings of the Followers of Ptolemy and Colorbasus

The followers of Ptolemy believe that Bythos had two partners, which they call "affections" or emotions: Thought (Ennoea) and Will (Thelesis). They say that first, Bythos had the idea to create something, and then he chose to act on it. These two forces—his thought and will—interacted with each other, and from that came Monogenes (the Only-Begotten) and Aletheia (Truth). These two beings were meant to be visible images of the Father's inner thoughts and intentions. Monogenes came from the will and is male, while Aletheia came from thought and is female. So, Will became a kind of helper to Thought. Thought always longed to create, but she couldn't do it alone. When Will joined her, she was able to give birth to what she had imagined.

But these made-up stories about invisible beings remind me of the character Zeus from Homer's poems—he stayed up all night worrying about how to honor Achilles and destroy the Greeks. You can see that these fictional beings aren't wiser than the real God of the universe. The true God doesn't have to struggle with plans. When He thinks, He acts. When He wants something, it happens. His thinking and His will are one and the same. He is full of wisdom, power, light, sight, hearing—He is the source of every good thing.

Some of their so-called experts, especially those who follow Colorbasus, teach a different version. They say that the first eight Aeons (the Ogdoad) weren't created one at a time, but all at once by the First Father (Propator) and His Thought (Ennoea). Colorbasus talks about this as confidently as if he had been there when it happened. He and his group also say that Man (Anthropos) and Church (Ecclesia) didn't come from Word (Logos) and Life (Zoe), like others believe. Instead, they claim that Logos and Zoe came from Anthropos and Ecclesia.

They explain it this way: when the First Father thought about creating, he became known as "Father." Since what he created was true, it was called "Truth" (Aletheia). When he wanted to reveal himself, he was called "Man" (Anthropos). And when he actually brought forth what he had thought about, that was called "Church" (Ecclesia). Man spoke and created Word (Logos), who is the firstborn Son. Then Life (Zoe) came after Word. In this way, they say, the first Ogdoad was completed.

They also argue among themselves about who the Savior really is. Some say He came from all the Aeons combined, and because of this, He's called Eudocetos, which means "well-pleasing one," since all the spiritual beings were happy to glorify the Father through Him. Others say He was made only from the ten Aeons that came from Logos and

Zoe, and that's why He's called Logos and Zoe, to honor His origins. Others claim He came from the twelve Aeons that came from Man and Church, and that's why He's called the Son of Man—because He descended from Anthropos. Another group says He was made by Christ and the Holy Spirit, who were created to protect the Pleroma, and that's why He is called Christ, to reflect His source.

And yet another group says that the ultimate source of everything—called the First Father, or Proarche, or Prothought (Proanennoetos)—is actually Man (Anthropos). They claim this is the deepest secret of all: that the highest power, who contains everything, is named Anthropos. This, they say, is why the Savior calls Himself the "Son of Man."

Chapter XIII

The Deceptive Tricks and Evil Actions of Marcus

There's another man among the heretics named Marcus. He claims he has improved on what his teacher taught, but he's really just skilled at fake miracles and magic tricks. Because of this, he's fooled many people—especially women—into following him. They believe he has deep wisdom and great power from mysterious spiritual realms. He acts like someone sent ahead of the Antichrist. By mixing the tricks of a stage performer with magical acts, his confused followers think he performs real miracles.

He pretends to bless wine during ceremonies, saying long prayers over it, until the wine appears to turn red or purple. He tells people this change means Charis—a heavenly power—is dropping her own blood into the cup. Then, people are told they should drink from it to receive Charis into themselves. He even gets women to perform the blessing over wine while he watches. After they do this, he brings out a larger cup and pours the smaller one into it. Then he says things like, "May the Charis who is above all things and beyond understanding fill your soul, and grow inside you like a mustard seed in good soil." While saying things like this, he pretends to do a miracle when the big cup overflows with wine from the smaller one. He uses tricks like these to completely fool people and gain their trust.

It seems very likely that Marcus uses a demon to help him. Through it, he acts like he can predict the future and lets others—whom he chooses—believe they're prophets too. He targets wealthy, well-dressed, upper-class women and tries to win them over with flattering and seductive words. He says things like, "I want to share my Charis with you, because the Father sees your angel always before Him. Your angel is among us now. Let us become one. Receive Charis from me. Dress like a bride waiting for her groom. Become what I am, and I'll become what you are. Make room in your soul for light. Take a spouse from me and be joined to him, while he also receives you. Look, Charis is coming down upon you. Open your mouth and prophesy."

If the woman answers, "I've never prophesied before, and I don't know how," Marcus will say more strange things to confuse and excite her. Then he'll tell her, "Just open your mouth and say whatever comes to mind—you'll be prophesying." At that point, the woman—now worked up and flattered, her heart racing—speaks nonsense, thinking it's divine prophecy. She becomes proud and thinks she's now a prophetess. She thanks Marcus for giving her Charis and tries to pay him back—not only with her wealth, but even by giving herself to him. She wants to be completely joined with him in every way.

Thankfully, some godly women who feared the Lord didn't fall for his lies. Marcus tried to seduce them too and told them to prophesy, but they saw through his deception. They knew that the true gift of prophecy comes only from God—not from Marcus or any magician.

True prophecy happens when and where God chooses, not when Marcus tells someone to speak. The one who gives orders is greater than the one being commanded. So if Marcus—or anyone—can order someone to prophesy, that would make him greater than the prophetic spirit, which is clearly wrong. The spirits that obey Marcus or his followers aren't from God—they're weak, fake, and rebellious. They come from Satan to mislead those who don't stay faithful to the teachings they first received from the Church.

Some women who were tricked by Marcus have returned to the Church. They admitted that he used magic potions and love charms to seduce them. They confessed they were overwhelmed by passion and defiled by him. One sad case involved a deacon from Asia who let Marcus stay in his home. Marcus seduced his wife, who was a beautiful woman. She ended up following Marcus for a long time, both emotionally and physically. After the Church helped bring her back, she spent her days confessing her sins and mourning the damage Marcus had caused her.

Some of Marcus' students also copied his actions. They tricked and seduced foolish women, leading them into sin. These men claimed to be "perfect," acting like no one—not even Paul, Peter, or the other apostles—knew as much as they did. They believed they alone had received the deep knowledge of the "unspeakable" power. They said they were above all authority and could do whatever they wanted. They believed they were untouchable and invisible to any judge because of something they called "Redemption."

Even if they were caught, they said they could just say a few magic words and be saved. They recited things like: "O you who sit beside God, next to the eternal mystery called Silence, the one who leads the angels that always see the Father's face—those angels take their form through you. Because of the kindness of the First Father, you created us as reflections of them. Now the judge is calling me to answer for myself. But you, who know everything, speak for both of us—it's really just one cause." After saying this, they believe the Mother puts an invisible helmet on them so the judge can't see them. Then she lifts them up, brings them into a secret wedding room, and unites them with their spiritual partners.

In our own region near the Rhône River, these false teachings have led many women astray. Some were so deeply tricked that their consciences felt dead, as if burned. A few have publicly admitted what they did. Others are too ashamed to speak up, and now live in silence, feeling hopeless about ever receiving God's life again. Some have even completely walked away from their faith. Others are stuck in the middle, unsure whether to return or walk away—lost and confused, as if they've been poisoned by the so-called "knowledge" these heretics promised.

Chapter XIV

The Strange Theories of Marcus About Letters and Sounds

Marcus claimed he alone was the container of the secret silence (Sige) of Colorbasus, calling himself the only one born to hold it. He said that a powerful group of four divine beings (the Tetrad) came down to him from mysterious, invisible places in the form of a woman—because the world couldn't handle them in male form. This being, he said, revealed the origin of everything only to him, something no god or person had ever been told before.

According to Marcus, in the beginning, the uncreated, unknowable Father, who had no body and was neither male nor female, wanted to express something that couldn't be spoken. So, He opened His mouth and released a Word just like Himself. That Word stood beside Him and revealed His nature. Then the Father spoke His name in four stages. The first sound had four letters, the second had four more, the third had ten, and the fourth had twelve. Altogether, that made thirty letters and four separate sounds.

Marcus said each part of this name had its own shape, sound, and meaning, but none of the parts could fully understand the others or even itself. Each one thought it was the full name, continuing to speak until it reached its final sound. He believed that when all these parts are finally united and make the same sound together, everything will be restored. He thought the word Amen symbolized this unity because everyone says it together. He also believed the different sounds made up the invisible spiritual world and were the forms that God called angels—beings who always look at the face of the Father.

He said these letters and sounds—sometimes called Aeons, words, seeds, or fruits—were all summed up in the name Ecclesia (the Church). According to him, the last letter of the last sound created its own elements in the image of the ones before it, which gave order to the universe and brought spiritual things into being. Marcus claimed that each of these letters held other letters inside, like layers, each spelling out more names. For example, the letter D in the word Delta is written with other letters (D-E-L-T-A), and each of those has more letters inside them. So, he believed the letters keep multiplying forever.

He taught that the Father knew His nature was too great to be fully understood, so He allowed each letter (or Aeon) to express just one part of His name, since none of them could speak the whole thing alone.

The Tetrad, continuing her explanation to Marcus, said, "Now I will show you Truth herself. I brought her down from above so you can see her clearly and admire her wisdom." She then described Truth's body in terms of Greek letters: her head is Alpha and Omega, her neck is Beta and Psi, her shoulders and hands are Gamma and Chi, and so on, down to her feet, which are Mu and Nu. This strange combination of letters, Marcus claimed, formed the "body of Truth." He called this being Anthropos (Man), the source of all speech and the voice of silent Sige. He told his followers to lift their thoughts high and listen to the divine Word spoken by Truth.

Then, according to Marcus, Truth looked at him, opened her mouth, and said one word: Christ Jesus. After that, she became silent again. Marcus waited for more, but then the Tetrad told him, "You think that name is simple and common, but you don't understand its true meaning. You only know how it sounds, not the power behind it. The name Jesus has six letters and is familiar to many. But in the higher realms, that name has many parts and is known differently by the angels connected to Him."

Marcus explained that the 24 letters in the Greek alphabet represent three divine powers. The nine silent (mute) letters symbolize the Father and Truth, since they can't be spoken. The seven semi-vowels stand for Word (Logos) and Life (Zoe), since they are between vowels and consonants. The eight vowels represent Man (Anthropos) and Church (Ecclesia), since human voice gave them shape. Logos and Zoe get eight letters, Anthropos and Ecclesia get seven, and the Father and Truth get nine. Because the groups had unequal numbers, Marcus said a divine being came from the Father to balance them all, so each group would have eight letters. These three balanced groups formed 24 letters total.

Then, by using his own logic, Marcus said that if you add special "double" letters (like ones with two sounds), the total becomes 30.

These, he claimed, match the total number of Aeons, which the ineffable Tetrad created through speech.

Marcus taught that the meaning of all this was shown through Jesus. After six days, He climbed a mountain with three others, becoming the sixth. Then, like the eighth (Ogdoad), He descended, showing He contained all things. He said the dove that came down during Jesus' baptism (which equals 801 in Greek numbers) proved this mystery. Moses also said man was made on the sixth day, and Jesus died on the sixth day and sixth hour—marking the new birth of humanity. Marcus believed this proved the number six meant both creation and rebirth.

He even said the special "double" letters hold the number six, and when added to the alphabet, they create 30 letters, revealing Jesus' name.

According to the silence (Sige) of Marcus, seven special letters show the free will of a lower being named Achamoth. She says, "This new six-letter figure, cut and separated, created the world through his own power. It has seven parts and is the soul of all visible things. He uses this world freely, while the rest serve the hidden desire of the Mother." Each of the seven heavens speaks a different vowel: the first says Alpha, the second Epsilon, the third Eta, the fourth (middle one) Iota, the fifth Omicron, the sixth Upsilon, and the seventh says Omega. These sounds, she claimed, praise the one who created them, and that praise rises up to the Father. That same praise, carried down to earth, created the world.

He even claimed that newborn babies cry out using these sounds, praising the Word just like the seven heavenly powers. That's why, he said, David wrote, "Out of the mouths of babies, You have made perfect praise." He also said the soul, when in pain, cries out "O," as if calling for help from its higher self.

In the end, Marcus claimed that all of this—the 30-letter name, the silent Father (Bythus), the 12-part body of Truth, and the name that cannot be spoken—explains both the world and human souls. He said everything matches heavenly patterns. And now, to complete the story, he promised to show how the Tetrad revealed the matching power in numbers—so that none of his supposed knowledge would be hidden, and that every part of his teaching would be shared just as he claimed it was revealed to him.

Chapter XV

Sige Tells Marcus How the Twenty-Four Elements and Jesus Came to Be. These Claims Are Absurd.

The mysterious figure Sige told Marcus how the twenty-four elements came to be. She said that along with Monotes (Unity) existed Henotes (Oneness). From these came two more: Monas and Hen. When you add all four together, that makes two plus two, or four. Then, adding two and four gives six. When that six is multiplied by four, it becomes twenty-four. These twenty-four are said to be the forms or "elements."

Marcus claimed that the first four names are so holy that they can't be spoken and are only known by the Son and the Father. But the next group of four names—Arrhetos, Sige, Pater, and Aletheia—can be said out loud with respect. Counting the letters in these names: Arrhetos has 7, Sige has 5, Pater has 5, and Aletheia has 7, which adds up to 24. He also said the next group—Logos, Zoe, Anthropos, and Ecclesia—works the same way. According to Marcus, the name "Jesus" has six letters, but His secret, unspoken name has twenty-four. The phrase "Christ the Son" has twelve letters, and the hidden version of this name has thirty. He said this is why Jesus is called the Alpha and Omega—like the dove, which supposedly also equals 801 in number value.

Marcus also claimed that Jesus has a special origin. From the first group of four came a second group, making a total of eight (an "Ogdoad"). Then a group of ten ("Decad") came next. Eight times ten is eighty, and then multiplying that eighty by ten again makes 800. When you add all the letters from the eight times ten pattern, you get 888, which he said is the number for Jesus. The Greek alphabet was used to support this idea—eight single letters, eight sets of tens, and eight sets of hundreds, totaling 888. Because of this, Marcus said Jesus is the total of all numbers, the Alpha and Omega.

Marcus also added that when you count up the first four numbers—one, two, three, and four—you get ten. He said that this number also means Jesus. The name "Christ" has eight letters, which stands for the Ogdoad. Multiply that by ten and you get Jesus (888). He also said that "Christ the Son" is really the "Duodecad" (meaning 12). The word "Son" has four letters and "Christ" has eight, adding up to twelve.

Before this name appeared, Marcus said people lived in deep ignorance. But when Jesus appeared in human form, with six letters in His name and twenty-four total, people came to know Him. Through this, they moved from death to life. He claimed this knowledge helped them reach the Father, who wanted to end ignorance and destroy death. So God chose a man (Anthropos) made in the image of this divine power to carry out this plan.

The Aeons came from the original group of four—Anthropos, Ecclesia, Logos, and Zoe. From these powers, Jesus was created to live on earth. The angel Gabriel stood in for Logos, the Holy Spirit stood for Zoe, the Power of the Highest represented Anthropos, and Mary stood in for Ecclesia. By this plan, Jesus was born through Mary, and through Him people could come to know the Father.

At His baptism, a dove came down—this represented a being who had gone up before and now came back down. That being held the seed of others like Him and went up and down with Him. Marcus claimed this power was from the Father and contained the Father, the Son, and Sige's power, which cannot be spoken out loud. This same power was also said to hold all the Aeons. This was the Spirit who spoke through Jesus and revealed both the Father and the Son. He said Jesus, formed by this plan, ended death, and Christ revealed the Father.

So, according to Marcus, Jesus was formed after the heavenly man (Anthropos) and, once He received the divine Aeon, He held within Himself all the heavenly beings: Anthropos, Logos, Pater, Arrhetos, Sige, Aletheia, Ecclesia, and Zoe.

This teaching is wild and hard to take seriously. Marcus makes the truth sound like a puppet covered in letters. He ignores history, claiming the truth came only after Greek letters were invented. The Greeks say Cadmus gave them the first sixteen letters, and others added new ones over time. If Marcus is right, then truth didn't even exist before those letters were invented—making it younger than Cadmus, the alphabet, and even Marcus himself.

Who could accept Marcus' idea that Sige—who supposedly can't speak—somehow explained the nature of a God who is too great to be explained? He says God opened His mouth and spoke a Word made up of four syllables and thirty parts, as if God were just another creature. If that's true, then God is made up of letters and syllables just like His Word. Marcus turns God, the Creator of all things, into a math puzzle of syllables, letters, and made-up heavenly math.

Marcus builds his version of God with letters and sounds. He says the Father has no body or form, yet describes Him using numbers and made-up words. He even claims the Father is made up of mute letters, consonants, and vowels—things made by people! He's leading his followers into foolishness and even blasphemy.

That's why an elder of the church once said in a poem:

Marcus, builder of false gods,

Watcher of signs in the sky,

Master of tricks and dark magic,

Using lies to spread false beliefs,

Showing fake miracles to fool your followers,

Powered by Satan through the fallen angel Azazel,

You are paving the way for Satan's wicked plans.

I'll now try to summarize the rest of Marcus' complicated teachings quickly so they can be clearly understood and easier to refute.

Chapter XVI

Foolish Ideas from the Followers of Marcus

Some of Marcus' followers try to mix their own strange beliefs about heavenly beings with the story Jesus told about the lost sheep. They think they are being deep or mystical, but really they just obsess over numbers. They claim the whole universe came from the numbers one and two. From there, they count up to four, and then add one, two, three, and four together to get ten. That gives them the idea of ten heavenly beings. Then they double the number two to get two, four, and six, which adds up to twelve. That becomes their idea of twelve heavenly powers.

If they keep counting this way up to ten, they reach thirty, which they say includes the numbers eight, ten, and twelve. They call this group of twelve "the suffering group" because they say one of them messed up and caused a problem. That's why, they claim, the sheep in Jesus' story ran off—it represents the failure of one of these twelve. They also say that when one of the twelve powers left, it was like the woman in Jesus' parable who lost a coin and lit a lamp to find it. So, they point out that the woman had nine coins left, and there were eleven sheep left—multiply nine by eleven, and you get ninety-nine. They say this is a hidden meaning in the word "Amen," since the letters of that word add up to ninety-nine in Greek.

They also claim the Greek letter Eta, along with another special symbol called Episemon, equals eight. Eta is the eighth letter, so they say that means it has something to do with the number thirty. If you add up the values of the letters from Alpha to Eta, skipping Episemon, they say it equals thirty. So they call thirty "the wonderful number." They say this group of thirty heavenly powers came from combining smaller groups of eight, ten, and twelve. When you multiply three by thirty, you get ninety, and if you multiply three by three, you get nine. So according to them, the group of eight creates ninety-nine this way.

They also focus on the Greek letter Lambda, which is the eleventh letter. They say that when the twelfth heavenly power failed, only eleven were left, so Lambda came down looking for another to complete the group again. They say the letter Mu (which looks like two Lambdas) shows this reunion. So now they try to avoid staying stuck at the number ninety-nine—which they say stands for failure—and aim to add one more to reach one hundred, which they call "the right side."

I know you're probably laughing at how ridiculous this all sounds. But it's also very sad. These people treat religion like a numbers game and pull apart the amazing truth about God just to fit their weird ideas using the alphabet. They twist God's real plan into made-up nonsense.

Paul warned us not to listen to people like this and told us to stay away from them after we've warned them once or twice. And the apostle John said we shouldn't even say hello to such people, because doing so makes us part of their evil behavior. He was right—there's no "good luck" or blessing for people who go against God.

These people are extremely disrespectful. They claim the one true God, the Creator of everything, came from a mistake—and not even the first mistake, but the third one! That's not just wrong—it's dangerous. We should avoid these people completely.

And the more they talk about their so-called "knowledge" and take pride in it, the more obvious it becomes that something dark is at work in them. They remind me of people who are sick but think they're fine—who laugh and act like everything is normal, when really they're in serious trouble. That's how these people are. The more they act like they're wiser than everyone else, the more foolish they really are.

The truth is, they've opened themselves up to evil spirits. When the spirit of foolishness leaves someone, and that person doesn't turn to God but focuses only on strange teachings, more evil spirits come in and take over. Marcus and his followers are so caught up in themselves that they've become full of these "eight evil spirits of foolishness."

Chapter XVII

The Marcosians' Idea That the World Was Made as a Copy of Invisible Things

They also teach a strange idea about how the world was made. According to them, everything in creation was formed by the mother through a lower god (whom they call the Demiurge), and he did it without even knowing he was copying something higher and invisible.

First, they say the four elements—fire, water, earth, and air—are copies of a higher group of four heavenly beings. Then they add the effects of these elements—heat, cold, dryness, and moisture—which gives a total of eight, matching what they call the Ogdoad (a heavenly group of eight).

Next, they describe ten powers, like this: seven are round bodies they call the heavens, the eighth is the shell or outer sky that holds them all, and the last two are the sun and the moon. These ten, they say, represent a heavenly group of ten that came from Logos (Word) and Zoe (Life).

The twelve signs of the zodiac, they claim, are images of another group of twelve heavenly beings, the children of Anthropos (Man) and Ecclesia (Church). They say the highest heaven moves quickly and helps control the entire system of stars, completing one full circle in thirty years. They say this circular path is a symbol of Horus, going around his mother who has thirty names (meaning the group of thirty heavenly powers).

Then they point to the moon, which completes its path in thirty days, as another symbol of the group of thirty. They even say the sun, which finishes its path in twelve months, shows the group of twelve, and each day, with twelve hours, is also a symbol of the twelve. Going further, they claim that each hour has thirty parts, which again reflects the group of thirty. And since the zodiac circle has 360 degrees (because each of the twelve signs has thirty degrees), this circle also shows the connection between the twelve and the thirty.

They say the Earth is divided into twelve zones. Each one, they believe, receives energy from the heavens based on where the sun is directly above it. The plants and life that grow there, they claim, reflect the heavenly group of twelve and its children.

They also say the lower god (the Demiurge) wanted to copy the higher realm's infinite, eternal, and limitless nature. But because he came from a flaw or mistake, he couldn't really do it. So instead, he tried to fake it by spreading out time into years, seasons, and ages. He thought that using a huge number of years would make it seem eternal.

But they say he missed the truth and chased something false. And that's why, when time runs out, everything he made will also come to an end.

Chapter XVIII

How the Heretics Twist Moses' Writings to Support Their Theories

These people come up with new ideas all the time, each trying to outdo the other by inventing more strange teachings. They believe no one among them is "perfect" unless they create some new, wild idea. So, I'll first explain how they misuse the writings of Moses and then show why their ideas are wrong.

They claim that the way Moses begins the story of creation proves their own beliefs. When Moses wrote, "In the beginning God created the heavens and the earth," they say the words "God," "beginning," "heavens," and "earth" stand for their group of four heavenly beings, called a Tetrad. When Moses describes the earth as "formless and empty," they say this shows that these beings are hidden and hard to understand.

Then, when Moses talks about the deep waters, darkness, and the Spirit moving over the waters, they say this refers to a second group of four that came from the first. They also say that Moses described a group of ten when he named ten things in creation: light, day, night, sky, evening, morning, dry land, sea, plants, and trees.

The number twelve, they say, shows up when Moses mentions the sun, moon, stars, seasons, years, big sea creatures, fish, reptiles, birds, four-legged animals, wild animals, and finally, humans. That makes twelve, which they say stands for another heavenly group of twelve. Together, these add up to the thirty beings they say rule the invisible world.

They also claim that humans were made to reflect these heavenly powers. They say the brain holds four special abilities—sight, hearing, smell, and taste—that match the heavenly four. Then they say people have eight features—two eyes, two ears, two nostrils, and a twofold sense of taste (sweet and bitter)—to show the number eight. Fingers make ten, which represents the group of ten, and they split the human body into twelve parts to match the twelve heavenly beings. The group of eight, they say, is hidden inside the body where it can't be seen.

They also point out that the sun was created on the fourth day and say that proves the number four is special. The clothes of the priest in the Old Testament, with four colors and four rows of jewels, also, they claim, reflect this number. They find anything in the Bible that connects to the number four and say it supports their belief.

They say man was made on the eighth day (or sometimes the sixth, depending on how they explain it), and this shows something important about the number eight. Some even believe there were two different creations of man—one spiritual and one physical.

They say that when eight people were saved in Noah's ark, it showed that salvation comes from the number eight. They say David being the eighth son proves this too. They even say that circumcision on the eighth day is a sign of the heavenly eight. Basically, anything they find with the number eight, they connect to their idea of a special group of eight divine powers.

When it comes to the number ten, they point to the ten nations God promised Abraham, and how Sarah gave Hagar to Abraham after ten years. They mention the ten gold bracelets given to Rebekah, Rebekah's family asking her to stay for ten days, Jeroboam getting ten tribes, the ten sections in the temple, the ten-foot-high columns, and the ten sons of Jacob who went to Egypt for food. They even say the ten apostles who first saw Jesus after His resurrection (without Thomas) represent the heavenly group of ten.

For the number twelve, they say the twelve sons of Jacob, the twelve tribes of Israel, the twelve stones on the high priest's breastplate, the twelve stones set up by Moses and Joshua, the twelve who carried the ark, the twelve stones Elijah used, and the twelve apostles all reflect the group of twelve. Basically, if there's a "twelve" in the Bible, they say it's about their heavenly twelve.

Then, when you add all these numbers together—four, ten, and twelve—you get thirty, which they call the Triacontad. They try to prove this number by saying Noah's ark was thirty cubits tall, that Samuel seated Saul among thirty guests, that David hid in the field for thirty days and had thirty warriors, and that the tabernacle was thirty cubits high. Any number that matches thirty, they say, proves their idea of the thirty heavenly powers.

Chapter XIX

Bible Verses They Twist to Claim That the True Father Was Unknown Before Christ.

They also try to use Bible verses to convince people that the highest God—their so-called "First Father"—was completely unknown until Jesus came. They say that before Christ, no one had any idea about this invisible Father, whom they call the "Propator." By doing this, they try to claim that Jesus revealed a different Father than the God who created the world. As I mentioned earlier, they wrongly say the Creator came from some kind of mistake.

For example, when the prophet Isaiah says, "Israel doesn't know Me, and My people don't understand Me," they twist this to mean that people didn't know the invisible Bythus (which is another name they use for their unknown god). They also quote Hosea saying, "There is no truth or knowledge of God in them," and say this shows ignorance of Bythus too. Then they bring up the line, "No one understands or seeks after God; all have turned away and become useless," and say that's also about people not knowing their Bythus. Even the verse from Moses, "No one can see God and live," is taken by them as proof that the true God remained hidden.

They wrongly claim that the Creator was visible and that the prophets saw Him. So when the Bible says, "No one can see God and live," they argue this means no one can see the greater, invisible Father. But we know the verse is actually talking about the Creator Himself, who is the true and invisible God—not this made-up Bythus they talk about.

They also say that when Daniel asked the angels to explain visions and didn't understand them, it shows he didn't know the real Father. They point to the angel's words: "Go your way, Daniel, for these words are sealed until people with understanding will understand, and those who are purified will be made pure." Then they claim that they are the ones who are "pure" and have the special understanding the angel spoke about.

Chapter XX

The Fake Scriptures and Twisted Gospel Verses Used by the Marcosians

They don't just twist real Bible verses—they also use a huge number of fake and made-up writings that they themselves invented. These writings are meant to confuse simple-minded people or anyone who doesn't really know the true Scriptures. One of their made-up stories claims that when Jesus was a young boy learning the alphabet, His teacher told Him, "Say Alpha." Jesus said "Alpha." But when the teacher asked Him to say "Beta," Jesus supposedly replied, "You tell me what Alpha means first, and then I'll tell you what Beta means." They claim this shows Jesus had a secret knowledge of the unknown God and used "Alpha" to reveal that.

They also twist real verses from the Gospels to fit their false beliefs. For example, when Jesus was twelve years old and said to His mother, "Didn't you know I must be about my Father's business?" they claim He was talking about a different Father—the one nobody knew. They say this is why He sent the disciples to the twelve tribes: to tell them about this unknown God. When someone called Him "Good Teacher," and Jesus answered, "Why do you call Me good? There is only One who is good—the Father in heaven," they say "heaven" here actually means the Aeons, or spiritual beings.

They also say that when Jesus didn't answer those who asked, "By what power are you doing this?" but instead asked them a question in return, He was showing that the true Father couldn't be explained in words. When He said, "I often wanted to hear one of these words, but no one could say it," they say the "one" word means the one true God. And when He cried over Jerusalem and said, "If only you knew what brings peace—but now it's hidden from you," they say the word "hidden" points to the mysterious Bythus.

They also point to when Jesus said, "Come to Me, all you who are tired and burdened... learn from Me," claiming He was offering to teach them about the Father of truth—who they believe was previously unknown.

Their favorite verse—the one they claim is the most important proof of all—is when Jesus says, "I thank You, Father, Lord of heaven and earth, because You've hidden these things from the wise and smart people and revealed them to children. Yes, Father, because that's what You wanted. All things have been given to Me by My Father. No one knows the Son except the Father, and no one knows the Father except the Son—and those to whom the Son chooses to reveal Him."

They say this proves their idea that the Father of truth was completely unknown until Jesus came. They insist that the Creator of the world was already known by everyone, so these words couldn't have been about Him. Instead, they claim Jesus was revealing this hidden Father—the one they now preach.

Chapter XXI

What These Heretics Believe About Redemption

Their idea of "redemption" is confusing, unclear, and changes depending on who you ask. They say it comes from something invisible and impossible to understand, which is why no one explains it the same way. Everyone who teaches this has their own version, so there are as many versions of "redemption" as there are teachers. Later, we'll show how Satan led them to reject Christian baptism, which brings new life with God, and how that rejection turns them away from the entire Christian faith.

They claim that people who gain perfect knowledge must be "reborn" into a higher power—otherwise, they can't enter the spiritual realm, which they call the Pleroma. This rebirth, they say, takes people into the depths of Bythus. They believe that the baptism Jesus gave to people was only for forgiving sins, but that the deeper "redemption" came from the Christ who came down on Jesus, and this brought full spiritual growth. They call the first baptism "animal" and the second "spiritual." They say John's baptism was about turning away from sin, while Jesus' "redemption" was about reaching perfection. They even twist Jesus' words, "I have another baptism to undergo," to support their ideas.

They also point to the time when the mother of James and John asked Jesus if her sons could sit beside Him in His kingdom. When Jesus asked if they could be baptized with His baptism, they say He was talking about this special "redemption." They claim Paul also wrote about this "redemption in Christ Jesus," which they teach in many confusing and conflicting ways.

Some of them act out a ritual that looks like a spiritual wedding, saying it matches the heavenly pairings above. Others bring people to water and baptize them while saying things like, "In the name of the unknown Father of the universe, in the name of truth, in the name of the one who came down on Jesus, in the name of unity, redemption, and connection with the powers." Others speak strange Hebrew-like words to confuse people more: "Basema, Chamosse, Baoenaora, Mistadia, Ruada, Kousta, Babaphor, Kalachthei." They say these words mean something like: "I call on the highest power of the Father—light, good Spirit, and life—because You have ruled in the body."

Others explain redemption with phrases like: "The hidden name above all gods, that Jesus of Nazareth wore in the lives of light. Christ lives by the Holy Spirit for angelic redemption." Then they say a string of names that are supposed to have special power. Their meanings are things like: "I do not separate Christ's Spirit. I want to enjoy Your name, Savior of truth!" The person being initiated replies, "I'm saved, I've been set free. I free my soul from this world and everything in it, in the name of Iao, who freed His own soul in Christ." Others around them say, "Peace to all who carry this name." After that, they anoint the person with perfume, saying it stands for a sweet smell from the higher world.

Some say water isn't needed at all. Instead, they mix oil and water and pour it on the person's head while saying special words. Others skip the rituals completely and say it's wrong to use physical things like water and oil to represent spiritual truths. They believe that simply knowing the truth about the invisible and powerful God is what saves you. According to them, sin and suffering come from ignorance, so learning the truth makes that all disappear. That knowledge is what they call true redemption. It isn't about the physical body, because the body dies. It's not about the "soul" either, since they say the soul comes from something broken. Instead, they say the "spirit" inside a person is saved through knowledge—and once you know everything, you don't need anything else. That, they claim, is true redemption.

Some go even further. They say people can be "redeemed" even right before they die by putting oil and water—or that same ointment—on their heads while saying those special words. They believe this makes the person invisible to the rulers and powers of the world. Their body stays behind, but their soul rises up to God. They're told that if they meet these spiritual rulers, they should say, "I come from the eternal Father. I'm His child. I've come to understand everything. These things aren't really anyone else's but come from Achamoth, who is female and made them for herself. I come from the eternal one, and I'm returning to where I belong."

Then, when they get closer to God, they're told to say, "I'm more valuable than the female who created you. If your mother doesn't know where she came from, I do. I call on the perfect wisdom, who is in the Father. She is the mother of your mother. She has no father or husband. She's a woman from a woman, and she made you even though she didn't know her own mother." They say when these rulers hear that, they get upset and blame their own source. Then the person, now "free," leaves behind their human nature.

These are the things we've heard about their version of redemption. But because they disagree so much and keep inventing new teachings all the time—especially the newer ones who just want to sound different—it's hard to describe everything they believe.

Translated by Tim Zengerink

Chapter XXII

How the Heretics Turn Away from the Truth

What we believe and teach as the truth is this: There is only one all-powerful God who created everything through His Word. He made the universe from nothing. The Scriptures clearly say, "The heavens were made by the Word of the Lord, and all their power by the breath of His mouth," and also, "All things were made through Him, and nothing was made without Him." This leaves no room for exceptions. The Father created everything through His Word—things we can see and things we can't, things that belong to this world and things that are eternal. He didn't use angels or separate powers to make these things. God didn't need any help. By His own Word and Spirit, He created, arranged, and ruled over everything. He brought everything into existence. He made the world and He made mankind. He is the God of Abraham, Isaac, and Jacob. There is no other God above Him—no other beginning, no other power, no higher reality. He is the Father of our Lord Jesus Christ, and we will show this clearly.

By holding on to this belief, we can easily show that these heretics have turned away from the truth, even though they have many different teachings. Most of them claim to believe in one God, but their ideas twist the truth, just like idol worshippers do. In doing this, they disrespect the One who made them. They speak against the work of God—especially against their own salvation—and end up accusing themselves. They lie about the truth and deny the one who can save them. But no matter how stubborn they are, one day they will rise again in their physical bodies and will have to admit the power of the One who raises the dead. However, because they refused to believe, they will not be counted among the righteous.

Because there are so many different heresies and false teachings, and each one is a bit different, we think it's important to explain their origin first. By understanding where their beliefs come from—especially their idea of a great and hidden "Bythus"—you'll be able to see how such strange and misleading teachings grew from that root.

Chapter XXIII

The Beliefs and Actions of Simon Magus and Menander

Simon the Samaritan was a magician. Luke, who followed the apostles, wrote about him, saying, "There was a man named Simon who had practiced magic in that city and fooled the people of Samaria. He claimed he was someone important, and everyone, from the smallest to the greatest, believed him. They said, 'This man is the great power of God.'" People respected him because he had amazed them with his magic for a long time.

Simon pretended to believe in Jesus, thinking the apostles were using magic to heal people and give them the Holy Spirit. When he saw them laying hands on believers and filling them with the Spirit, he offered them money, hoping to buy this power. But Peter told him, "May your money die with you, because you thought you could buy God's gift! You have no share in this because your heart is not right with God. I see that you are full of bitterness and caught in sin." Still, Simon didn't truly believe in God. Instead, he focused even more on magic so that people would continue thinking he was special. This happened during the rule of Claudius Caesar, who is said to have even honored Simon with a statue because of his so-called magical powers.

Simon was praised by many as if he were a god. He taught that he had appeared to the Jews as the Son, to the Samaritans as the Father, and to other people as the Holy Spirit. He claimed to be the highest of all powers—the Father of everything. He allowed people to call him by any title they liked.

Simon started a religious group based on these strange beliefs. He bought a woman named Helena, who was a slave in the city of Tyre, and traveled with her. He said she was the first thought that came from his mind and was the mother of everything. He taught that she helped him create angels and heavenly beings. According to Simon, Helena left him and went to the lower regions of space where she made angels and powers. But these angels became jealous and trapped her. They didn't know who Simon was and didn't want anyone to believe they came from anyone else. Helena was mistreated and couldn't return to Simon. Instead, she was stuck in human bodies for many years, moving from one woman to another. Simon even said she was the same Helen who caused the Trojan War. At one point, she became a prostitute. According to Simon, she was the "lost sheep" Jesus came to find.

Simon said that he came to rescue her first and also to save people by making himself known. He claimed that the angels who ran the world did a poor job because each one wanted to be in charge. So, he came to fix things. He disguised himself to look like other powers and angels, so people would think he was human, even though he wasn't. He said he only seemed to suffer in Judea, but really didn't. He also said that the Old Testament prophets were inspired by those same faulty angels, so his followers shouldn't listen to them. Instead, they should live however they want because salvation comes from Simon's grace—not from doing good deeds. He believed good and bad actions were just rules made up by the angels to control people. That's why he promised that the world would be destroyed and his followers would be freed from those angels' rule.

The leaders of Simon's group lived sinful lives and practiced all kinds of magic. They used spells, charms, potions, and summoned spirits and dream-figures. They even made statues of Simon and Helena to look like Jupiter and Minerva, and they worshiped them. This group became known as the Simonians, named after Simon. They were the first to spread what they called "secret knowledge," though it was really false.

Simon was followed by Menander, who was also from Samaria and skilled in magic. He taught that the highest power was still unknown to all, but he was the savior sent to free people. Like Simon, Menander said angels made the world, and they came from Ennoea, a thought or power. He claimed that through his magic, he could give people the knowledge they needed to defeat those angels. He told his followers that if they were baptized into him, they would rise again, never die, and stay forever young.

Chapter XXIV

The Teachings of Saturninus and Basilides

Saturninus, who was from Antioch near Daphne, and Basilides, who lived in Alexandria, both took advantage of the moment to create their own religious teachings. Saturninus, like Menander before him, taught that there was one invisible Father who no one really knew. This Father created angels, archangels, and other spiritual powers. He also said that a group of seven angels created the world and everything in it. According to him, humans were made by these angels too. He claimed that a glowing image came down from the highest power but quickly returned upwards, so the angels decided to make a man in their own image. They tried to shape him, but he couldn't stand upright because they didn't have enough power. The man crawled on the ground like a worm. Then, the higher power felt sorry for him and sent a spark of life that helped him stand up, join his body parts, and come to life. Saturninus believed that after death, this spark returned to where it came from, and the rest of the body just broke down into natural elements.

He also claimed that the Savior had no birth, no body, and no physical form. People only thought He looked like a man. He said the God of the Jews was just one of the angels, and that Christ came to destroy this angel and save those who had that divine spark. Saturninus was the first to say that angels created two types of people—some good, some evil—and that demons help the evil ones. So Christ came to destroy the demons and evil people while saving the good ones. They also said that marriage and having children were works of Satan. Many of Saturninus' followers avoided eating meat and pretended to be holy to attract followers. They believed some prophecies came from the angels who created the world, and others from Satan. Saturninus taught that Satan was actually one of these angels and the enemy of the world's creators, especially the God of the Jews.

Basilides tried to sound wiser by making his beliefs more complex. He said the first being born was "Nous" (mind), who came from the uncreated Father. From Nous came "Logos" (word), then "Phronesis" (wisdom), then "Sophia" (intelligence) and "Dynamis" (power). Sophia and Dynamis created spiritual rulers and angels, who made the first heaven. More angels came from them and made the second heaven, and so on. This pattern continued until there were 365 heavens. That's why, they claimed, there are 365 days in a year.

The angels in the lowest heaven—the one we can see—created everything on earth. They divided the earth and the nations among themselves. The leader of these angels, they said, was the God of the Jews. Since he wanted other nations to serve the Jews, the other angels fought against him, which is why the Jews were at odds with everyone else. The unseen Father, wanting to save people, sent His first-born,

Nous (who they also called Christ), to free believers from the control of these angels. According to them, Jesus came to earth as a man and performed miracles, but He never actually died. Instead, a man named Simon from Cyrene was forced to carry His cross and was made to look like Jesus. Simon was the one crucified while Jesus, who had taken Simon's appearance, watched and laughed. Because Jesus was really just a spirit, He could change form and disappear whenever He wanted. People who know this secret are supposedly free from the powers that made the world. They say we shouldn't honor the crucified man, but the one who only appeared to be crucified. If you believe in the one who was crucified, you are still a slave of the powers that made your body. But if you deny Him, then you are free and understand the true plan of the invisible Father.

They taught that salvation only belongs to the soul, because the body is naturally corrupt. Basilides said that the prophets got their messages from the angels who created the world, and that the law was given by their leader—the one who brought the Israelites out of Egypt. He didn't care whether people ate food sacrificed to idols and said it didn't matter. He believed anything could be done—including all kinds of immoral actions—because none of it mattered. His followers practiced magic and used spells, names of angels, and charms. They made up names for angels from different heavens and claimed to know all 365 levels and the beings in them. They said the secret name Jesus used to go up and down from heaven was "Caulacau."

Anyone who learns these things, they claimed, becomes invisible and untouchable, just like Caulacau. Just as no one knew who the Son was, these followers were supposed to be unknown to everyone else. They believed they could pass through all powers without being noticed. Their motto was, "Know everything, but let no one know you." Because of this, they could easily deny their beliefs when questioned—

they wouldn't suffer for their faith because they could blend in. They thought only a rare few—one in a thousand or two in ten thousand—could understand their teachings. They said they weren't Jews anymore, and not yet Christians either. They believed their secrets should never be spoken openly, but kept hidden in silence.

They placed their imaginary 365 heavens using ideas borrowed from mathematicians. They adapted mathematical theories into their strange beliefs. They also worshiped a being named Abraxas, claiming that name contains the number 365.

Chapter XXV

The Teachings of Carpocrates

Carpocrates and his followers believed that the world and everything in it was made by angels who were far beneath the highest God. They taught that Jesus was the son of Joseph and was just a regular man, except that His soul was pure and strong. Because of this, He could perfectly remember everything He had seen when He was close to the true God. For that reason, a special power came down from the Father and helped Jesus escape the control of the angels who made the world. That power passed through them all, remained free, and returned to the Father along with other souls that were similar to it. They also claimed that Jesus, although raised with Jewish customs, rejected them, and used special abilities to fight the sinful passions that exist as a punishment in people.

According to them, any soul that is like Christ's can reject the angels who made the world and gain the same power. This belief made them arrogant. Some even claimed to be equal to Jesus, while others said they were greater than His disciples, like Peter and Paul. They believed their souls came from the same place as His and that, since they too looked down on the world's creators, they deserved the same power and would return to the same place after death. And if someone rejected worldly things more than Jesus did, they considered that person even greater than Him.

They practiced magic, used spells and charms, and worked with spirits and demons said to bring dreams. They believed they could control not only the powers of this world but everything in it. These people, just like pagans, were influenced by Satan to make the church look bad. When people hear their teachings or see their actions, they may think all Christians are like them and turn away from the true message. But real believers have no connection to them—not in belief, not in behavior, and not in lifestyle. These heretics lived sinfully and used the name of Christ to hide their evil ideas. Because of this, their punishment from God is well deserved.

Their ideas were so extreme that they claimed they had the right to do anything—even the most sinful acts—because, they said, good and evil are just based on opinion. They believed that souls had to experience every kind of life and behavior by being born into different bodies over and over. The only exception would be if someone could live one life doing everything (even horrible things) all at once, so they wouldn't need to be reborn again. They said this was the only way to escape being stuck in this world. According to them, Jesus taught this idea secretly. They pointed to His words: "While you are on the way with your opponent, try hard to make peace, or he may hand you over to the judge, and the judge to the officer, and you be thrown into prison. You won't get out until you've paid the last penny." They claimed the "opponent" was an angel, the devil, who leads lost souls back to the high ruler. They said this devil is also the chief angel who helped make the world. He hands souls over to another angel who puts them into new bodies, which they called prisons.

So when Jesus said, "You won't get out until you've paid the last penny," they believed it meant that no one can escape the angels' control unless they go through every kind of experience on earth. Once the soul has done everything, it can finally be free and rise to the highest God, who is beyond the angels. That's how they said all souls are saved—either by doing everything in one lifetime or by being reborn again and again until they've done it all.

Because of this, they didn't consider evil actions to be truly evil. In their writings, they even said Jesus secretly taught His disciples these things and allowed them to pass them on to others who were faithful and worthy. They said salvation comes through faith and love, but everything else is neither good nor bad in itself—it's only considered good or bad depending on what people think.

Some of them marked their followers by branding the inside of their right ears. One of them, Marcellina, came to Rome during the time of Bishop Anicetus and led many people astray with these beliefs. They called themselves "Gnostics." They owned images—some painted, some made from different materials—and claimed that Pilate had a picture made of Jesus during His lifetime. They crowned these images and placed them alongside statues of philosophers like Pythagoras, Plato, and Aristotle. They even honored these images in ways similar to how pagans worship idols.

Chapter XXVI

The Teachings of Cerinthus, the Ebionites, and the Nicolaitans

Cerinthus was a man trained in Egyptian philosophy. He taught that the world wasn't created by the highest God, but by a lesser power, one that was far removed from the true Supreme Being and didn't even know that the highest God existed. Cerinthus also said that Jesus wasn't born from a virgin. Instead, he claimed Jesus was the natural son of Joseph and Mary, born like everyone else. Still, Jesus was better than other people—more moral, thoughtful, and wise. After Jesus was baptized, Cerinthus said that the Christ came down on Him like a dove, sent by the Supreme God. From that point on, Jesus began to teach about the unknown Father and perform miracles. But, according to Cerinthus, the Christ left Jesus before the crucifixion, so only Jesus suffered and rose again. Christ, being a spiritual being, was untouched by pain.

The group called the Ebionites also believed that God created the world, but their views about Jesus were similar to those of Cerinthus and Carpocrates. They only used the Gospel of Matthew and rejected the teachings of the Apostle Paul, saying that he abandoned the law of Moses. They also had unusual interpretations of the prophets and continued to follow Jewish laws like circumcision. Their lifestyle was so close to Judaism that they even treated Jerusalem as if it were God's home and worshiped it.

The Nicolaitans followed Nicolas, one of the seven men the apostles had chosen to help serve the church. However, his followers lived without self-control, giving in to every desire. Their behavior is clearly criticized in the Book of Revelation, where it says they believed it didn't matter if someone committed adultery or ate food offered to idols. That's why the Word says of them, "You hate the deeds of the Nicolaitans, which I also hate."

Chapter XXVII

The Teachings of Cerdo and Marcion

Cerdo followed the teachings of Simon and moved to Rome during the time of Bishop Hyginus, who was the ninth leader after the apostles. Cerdo taught that the God mentioned in the Jewish law and the writings of the prophets was not the same as the Father of Jesus Christ. He claimed the God of the Old Testament was known and strict, while the Father of Jesus was unknown and kind.

Marcion, who came from Pontus, built on Cerdo's teachings and took them even further. He claimed that the God described in the law and the prophets was the cause of evil, loved war, kept changing His mind, and even went against Himself. Marcion said that Jesus came from a different God, one who was higher than the Creator of the world. He said Jesus showed up in Judea during the rule of Pontius Pilate, looking like a man, and came to cancel the law, the prophets, and everything done by the Creator—whom Marcion called the "Cosmocrator," or ruler of the world.

Marcion changed the Gospel of Luke by removing the parts about Jesus' birth and taking out many teachings where Jesus clearly said the Creator of the universe was His Father. He told his followers that they should trust him more than the apostles who gave us the Gospel. Instead of giving them the full Gospel, he only shared parts of it. He also edited Paul's letters, cutting out every part that says the God who created the world is the Father of Jesus. Marcion even removed verses from the prophets that Paul used to show Jesus was the one they predicted would come.

According to Marcion, only the souls of people who believe his version of the truth will be saved. The body, he said, is made from the earth and can't be saved. He also said something completely backwards—like a voice speaking for the devil—that evil people like Cain, the people of Sodom, the Egyptians, and others who lived sinful lives were saved when Jesus went to the world of the dead (Hades). He claimed they ran to Him and welcomed Him. But he said that good people like Abel, Enoch, Noah, Abraham, the prophets, and all the righteous didn't get saved. Marcion taught that since they believed their God was always testing them, they thought Jesus was another test and didn't believe in Him. Because of that, he said their souls stayed in Hades.

Marcion is the only person known to have purposely and openly changed the Scriptures and insulted God so boldly. I plan to directly respond to him and prove he is wrong, using the very writings he claims to believe in—the teachings of Jesus and the apostles. For now, I've just mentioned him so that you know that anyone who twists the truth or damages the Church's message is really a follower of Simon Magus. Even if they don't admit it, they continue Simon's teachings. They use the name of Jesus like bait to trick people, but underneath, they spread Simon's false ideas. They hide poison under something that looks sweet and good, leading many people away from the truth.

Chapter XXVIII

Teachings of Tatian, the Encratites, and Others

Many new groups have broken off from the heresies already mentioned. This keeps happening because almost all of these people want to become teachers themselves. They leave the group they were in, create new ideas by mixing different beliefs, and then claim to have discovered something new. They insist on spreading their own opinions, no matter how strange they might be.

For example, a group called the Encratites, who came from the teachings of Saturninus and Marcion, preached against marriage. By doing this, they rejected the way God originally created people—male and female—to have children and grow the human race. Some of them also refused to eat meat, which showed they weren't thankful to God for creating all living things. They also claimed that Adam, the first man, could not be saved. But this idea didn't exist until a man named Tatian came along.

Tatian had once listened to Justin and followed his teachings. While Justin was alive, Tatian didn't teach these things. But after Justin's death, Tatian left the Church. He became proud and wanted to be seen as a leader. He started creating his own teachings. He made up a system that included invisible beings, like the ones Valentinus talked about. And like Marcion and Saturninus, Tatian said that marriage was evil and compared it to sin. The idea that Adam couldn't be saved was something Tatian made up himself.

There were also others who followed Basilides and Carpocrates. These people allowed sexual relationships with many partners and believed it was okay to have multiple wives. They didn't care about eating meat that had been offered to idols and said God didn't really care about such things.

There are too many of these groups to list them all. Each of them, in one way or another, has turned away from the truth.

Chapter XXIX

Doctrines of Various Other Gnostic Sects, and Especially of the Barbeliotes or Borborians

After the followers of Simon, many other Gnostic groups began popping up quickly, like mushrooms after rain. Here are some of the main ideas they believed in.

One group believed in a never-aging being called Barbelos, who lived in a pure and untouched spirit. They said there was an invisible Father who wanted to make Himself known to Barbelos. Then a thought, called Ennoea, came forward and asked the Father for the ability to see the future, called Prognosis. When that appeared, they asked for incorruptibility (called Aphtharsia), which also came, followed by eternal life (Zoe Aionios).

Barbelos became joyful and proud after receiving these gifts and created a light that was just like them. This light was, they believed, the beginning of everything. The Father blessed this light to make it perfect, and they said this was Christ. Christ asked for a helper named Nous (which means "mind"), and he appeared. Then the Father also sent Logos (meaning "word"). These figures were paired: Ennoea with Logos, Aphtharsia with Christ, Zoe Aionios with Thelema (meaning "will"), and Nous with Prognosis. All of them praised the great light and Barbelos.

Then they said that from Ennoea and Logos came a being called Autogenes, meaning "self-born." He was meant to represent the great light and was highly honored. Aletheia (which means "truth") was sent with him, and they were joined together. From Christ and Aphtharsia came four powerful lights that surrounded Autogenes. Then, from Thelema and Zoe Aionios came four more beings to serve the others.

They were called Grace (Charis), Will (Thelesis), Understanding (Synesis), and Wisdom (Phronesis). Grace was joined with the first light, who they named the Savior or Armogenes. Will was linked to the second, Raguel. Understanding to the third, David. Wisdom to the fourth, Eleleth.

Once all this was done, Autogenes created a perfect human named Adamas. They said he was undefeated, just like those he came from. He and the first light were separate from Armogenes. Autogenes also gave him perfect understanding so he could know the one above everything. The pure spirit gave him great strength. Everything inside him worshiped the eternal being. From him, they said, came the mother, father, and son. From Adamas and Gnosis (meaning "knowledge"), they said a special Tree was made, which they also called Gnosis.

Next, they claimed the Holy Spirit came from the first angel who stood beside the only-born one. They also called this Spirit Sophia or Prunicus. This Spirit noticed everyone else had a partner, but he didn't. So he looked for one, searching even in the lower worlds. Still not finding one, he got frustrated and jumped down without the Father's approval.

Because of his kindness and simple nature, he made something new, but it ended up including both ignorance and boldness. They said this creation was Protarchontes, the one who made the lower world. A powerful force took him from his mother and placed him far below, where he created the sky and lived in it. Confused, he made weaker beings—like angels, skies, and things on earth.

He joined with someone named Audacity (Authadia), and together they created Wickedness (Kakia), Jealousy (Zelos), Envy (Phthonos), Fury (Erinnys), and Lust (Epithymia). When these beings were created,

Sophia (his mother) became deeply sad and escaped to the higher realms, becoming the last of the eight divine beings, counting from the bottom up.

When she left, Protarchontes thought he was alone in the universe. That's why he said, "I am a jealous God, and there is no one else but me."

These are the strange and made-up beliefs that this group taught.

Chapter XXX

Doctrines of the Ophites and Sethians

Some groups claimed that from the power of a being named Bythus, there came a first light—blessed, pure, and endless. They called this being the First Man, or the Father of all. They said his thought (called Ennoea) came out from him and gave birth to a son, known as the Son of Man, or the Second Man. Beneath them was the Holy Spirit. Under the Holy Spirit, they believed, the basic elements like water, darkness, and chaos were separated. They said the Spirit floated above all this and called it the First Woman.

They said the First Man and his Son looked at the beauty of the Spirit (the woman), and by shining light on her, she gave birth to a third being—a light called Christ. He was said to be the child of the First Man, the Second Man, and the Spirit.

They taught that the Father and Son both united with the woman, whom they also called the Mother of the Living. But she couldn't hold their power, so she became overwhelmed and overflowed. Because of this, Christ, being part of the right side and aiming for higher things, was taken up along with his mother into a perfect, uncorrupted world.

This, they said, is the true Church, made up of the Father, the First and Second Man, Christ, and the Spirit.

Then they claimed that the overflow from the Spirit became sprinkled with light but fell downward. They called this being Sinistra, Prunicus, and Sophia. It was both male and female. This being went into the unmoving waters and stirred them up, acting freely and even recklessly. It took a body from the waters. All things were drawn to the light it carried. If it hadn't had that light, it would've been swallowed by the material world.

This being was now trapped in a heavy, physical body and regretted what it had done. It tried to rise back up to its mother but couldn't because the body was too heavy. It then tried to hide the light it carried to keep it safe from the lower elements. With some remaining power, it flew upward, stretched out, and formed the visible sky from its body. But it stayed under that sky, still in a watery form. Later, it longed again for the higher light and, gaining strength, threw off the body and became free. That body was then called "a female from a female."

They said that this being's son kept some of that pure breath from his mother and used it to act. He became strong and, they claimed, made a son of his own, but without a mother. Then that son made another son, and so on—until seven sons were made. The mother became the eighth. These sons each had their own rank and power.

They gave names to these beings. The first son was Ialdabaoth. His son was Iao. Then came Sabaoth, Adoneus, Eloeus, Oreus, and finally Astanphaeus. Each ruled in order over parts of heaven and earth. Ialdabaoth, the first, looked down on his mother and proudly made sons, grandsons, angels, and rulers without asking anyone's permission. But his sons began to fight with him for power, which made him very upset. He then focused on the lower world and created a son. This son, they said, became a twisted mind (Nous) in the shape of a serpent. From him came spirit, soul, and everything on earth—including forgetfulness, evil, jealousy, and death.

Because of all this, Ialdabaoth became proud and said, "I am the father and God, and there is no one above me." But his mother heard him and replied, "Don't lie, Ialdabaoth. The true Father and the original Man are above you, along with the Son of Man." When everyone heard this strange voice, they were confused and curious about where it came from. So Ialdabaoth, to take control again, said, "Let's make man in our image."

The six powers, along with their mother, created a huge human, shaped in length and width, based on her idea. But this human could only slither on the ground. They brought him to their father. Sophia was working to empty Ialdabaoth of his light so he couldn't challenge the higher powers. They say that when breath was put into the man, he gained intelligence and deep thought—these were the tools for salvation. Right away, this man thanked the true Father and turned away from his creators.

Ialdabaoth, now jealous, tried to weaken the man again by creating a woman from his own thoughts. But Prunicus secretly drained her power. When the other powers saw how beautiful she was, they called her Eve and fell in love with her. They had children with her—these, they said, were the angels. Then Sophia tricked Adam and Eve by using a serpent to get them to break Ialdabaoth's rule. Eve listened because she thought the serpent was a child of God and convinced Adam to eat the forbidden fruit too.

By eating it, they realized the truth and rejected their creators. When Prunicus saw that the powers had been beaten by their own creation, she was thrilled. She then declared that since the true Father cannot be corrupted, Ialdabaoth—who had claimed to be God—was a liar. She said that although the First Man and the First Spirit existed before, Eve had sinned by having a child outside of the true order.

Ialdabaoth, because he was still blinded by forgetfulness and didn't understand what was really happening, threw Adam and Eve out of Paradise when they disobeyed his command. He had wanted to have children with Eve but failed because his mother opposed him at every turn. She secretly removed the light from Adam and Eve—the divine light that came from the higher power—so that this spirit wouldn't be touched by any curse or shame from the fall. Once that light was gone, they say Ialdabaoth cursed them and sent them down to Earth.

The serpent, who was fighting against Ialdabaoth, was also cast down. But here in the lower world, the serpent gained control over the angels and had six sons, making himself the seventh—just like the group of seven (the Hebdomad) that surrounds the Father. These seven became known as the earthly demons. They always fight against humans because humans were the reason their father was thrown down.

Before the fall, Adam and Eve had bright, spiritual bodies. But once they entered this world, their bodies became heavier, duller, and slower. Their souls also weakened because they had only received a limited kind of spirit from their creator. Things stayed that way until Prunicus felt sorry for them and gave them back a touch of that divine light. With it, they remembered who they were. They realized they were naked and that their bodies were made of matter—which meant they carried death within them. They became patient, knowing this physical body was only temporary.

With Sophia's help, they learned how to find food. Once they were satisfied, they had children. Their first son was Cain. The serpent quickly took hold of Cain and filled him with forgetfulness and bold pride. Cain then killed his brother Abel, becoming the first to show jealousy and murder. Later, they say Prunicus helped bring about the birth of Seth and then Norea. All people came from them. But both the lower and higher Hebdomads pushed humanity toward evil—the lower by encouraging sin and the higher by promoting rebellion and idol worship. Meanwhile, the mother secretly protected what was hers: the divine light.

They also believed the seven stars, or planets, are the holy Hebdomad. The serpent who was cast down had two names: Michael and Samael.

Angry that people didn't worship him, Ialdabaoth sent a great flood to destroy them. But Sophia stopped him, and Noah and his family were saved through the power of the divine light. Humanity began again through them. Ialdabaoth later chose a man named Abraham and made a deal with him—if his descendants served Ialdabaoth, they would inherit the land. Later, through Moses, he led Abraham's descendants out of Egypt and gave them the Law, forming the Jewish people.

Among these people, he picked seven special days, which they called the holy Hebdomad. Each day had its own angel to praise God so that others would also follow these angels as gods, as announced by the prophets.

They divided the prophets into groups:

- Moses, Joshua, Amos, and Habakkuk belonged to Ialdabaoth.
- Samuel, Nathan, Jonah, and Micah to Iao.
- Elijah, Joel, and Zechariah to Sabaoth.
- Isaiah, Ezekiel, Jeremiah, and Daniel to Adonai.
- Tobias and Haggai to Eloi.

- Micaiah and Nahum to Oreus.
- Esdras and Zephaniah to Astanphaeus.

Each prophet praised their own god. They also believed Sophia herself spoke through some of these prophets, revealing truths about the first Man and Christ, and reminding people of the light and Christ's coming. The other powers were frightened by these messages. So Prunicus used Ialdabaoth—who didn't realize what he was doing—to bring about two miraculous births: one from Elizabeth (who had been unable to have children) and one from Mary, a virgin.

Because Prunicus had no peace anywhere, she cried out to her mother for help. Her mother, the first woman, felt compassion when she saw her daughter's sadness and asked the First Man to send Christ to help. Christ came down to join his sister Sophia and the divine light. When he saw her, he announced his coming through John and prepared the way with a baptism of repentance. He chose Jesus in advance, so that when Christ came, he would find a pure person to enter—and through Jesus, the woman (Sophia) would be revealed.

They claimed Christ came down through the seven heavens, taking on the appearance of each heavenly being to avoid detection. He drained their powers and attracted all the scattered divine light. When he reached Earth, he first gave this light to Sophia. Together, they rejoiced in being reunited. They described this as a celebration between bride and groom.

Jesus, born of Mary through God's power, was wiser, purer, and more righteous than anyone else. Christ, united with Sophia, entered into Jesus—making him Jesus Christ.

They believed most of Jesus's followers didn't realize that Christ had entered into him. Once Christ did, Jesus began to heal, perform miracles, and reveal the unknown Father. He openly called himself the

Son of the First Man. But the powers and Jesus's original father (Ialdabaoth) were angry and plotted to kill him.

When Jesus was taken away, Christ and Sophia left his body and returned to the perfect realm. Jesus was crucified alone. But Christ didn't forget him. He sent a power back into Jesus's body that brought him back to life—not in a regular body, but in a spiritual one. The parts of his body that were earthly went back to the world.

When the disciples saw him alive again, they didn't recognize him—not even Jesus himself knew how he had risen. They said this was a huge mistake among the disciples: they thought he had risen in a regular body, not realizing that "flesh and blood cannot enter God's kingdom."

They tried to prove that Christ came down from heaven and later went back up by pointing out that Jesus didn't perform any miracles before his baptism or after he rose from the dead. They said this was because people didn't realize that Jesus had been joined with Christ, and that the eternal Christ had temporarily connected with the seven rulers of this world (the Hebdomad). They claimed Jesus's earthly body was like that of an ordinary animal.

After Jesus rose from the dead, they said he stayed on Earth for eighteen months. During that time, divine knowledge came down to him from above, and he began to teach more clearly. He shared these deep secrets only with a few close followers—those he believed were smart enough to understand them. Then he returned to heaven.

They said Christ went up and sat at the right hand of his father, Ialdabaoth, without his father realizing what was happening. From that place, Christ would welcome the souls of those who truly understood the secret truths, once they left their physical bodies. As Christ received more and more of these pure souls, Ialdabaoth became weaker. This was because his power was slowly being drained, since those souls would no longer return to Earth—only the ones that belonged to him (those made from his own breath) could be sent back. Everything would eventually be complete when all the divine sparks of light were gathered together and brought into a perfect and unchanging heavenly world.

These strange beliefs came from the followers of Valentinus, and they spread many versions—like a beast with many heads. Some of them even said that Sophia (Wisdom) became the serpent in Eden. That's why she fought against the god who created Adam and gave humans knowledge. That's also why the serpent was called the wisest creature.

They also believed our intestines—the way they twist and carry food—were shaped like a serpent and showed that a hidden, snake-like source of life was inside us.

Chapter XXXI

Teachings of the Cainites

Some people claim that Cain came from a higher spiritual power and not from the Creator of the world. They believe that people like Esau, Korah, and the people of Sodom are spiritually connected to them. Because of this, they say the Creator tried to attack them, but none of them were truly harmed. They claim that Sophia (Wisdom) took back what belonged to her from them. They even say that Judas, the one who betrayed Jesus, understood these hidden truths better than anyone else. They believe he carried out the betrayal on purpose to fulfill a greater mystery, and that through his actions, both heaven and earth were shaken. They've written a made-up book about this story, which they call the Gospel of Judas.

I've collected some of their writings, and in them, they try to get rid of the laws created by someone they call Hystera—who they believe made heaven and earth. Like Carpocrates, they say that no one can be saved unless they experience every kind of sin. They even believe that an angel watches over them during their sinful acts and pushes them to be bold and unclean. Whatever evil they do, they say things like, "Angel, I'm doing your work," or "Power, I'm carrying out your task!" They claim this is what it means to have "perfect knowledge," even though they proudly do things too shameful to even talk about.

I thought it was important to clearly show how the followers of Valentinus come from these kinds of false teachings and misguided people. By explaining their beliefs, I hope that some of them might repent and turn back to the one true God, who made everything. I also hope that others won't get tricked into following these false teachers, thinking they'll learn some deeper secret or higher truth. Instead, people should learn from us how false and empty these ideas are. They should reject them and feel compassion for those still trapped in these made-up stories, who now act arrogantly as if they know more than everyone else—when really, they don't know anything at all. Just by showing what they believe, we've already shown how wrong they are.

That's why I worked hard to bring their hidden teachings into the open. Once their lies are exposed, we don't need to say much more to prove them wrong. It's like hunting a wild animal hiding in the woods. Once the beast is forced out into the open, you don't need to chase it yourself—others can see it, protect themselves, and attack it until it's defeated. In the same way, since we've revealed their secrets, everyone can now recognize and fight against their false teachings.

So, as I promised, I will keep going and do my best to refute them clearly in the next part of this work. Just talking about them takes a lot of effort, as you can see. But I'll give you everything you need to fight back against their twisted beliefs and replace them with the truth. I'll challenge each of their ideas in the order they were described, so that I don't just show the monster, but help you strike it down from every angle.

Thank You for Reading

Dear Reader,

We hope this timeless classic has sparked your imagination and enriched your literary journey. Now that you've turned the final page, we want to share a vision for the future of reading—one where every classic you've ever wanted to explore is at your fingertips, in a format that best suits your life.

We'd like to invite you to gain immediate, unlimited digital & audiobook access to hundreds of the most treasured literary classics ever written—along with the option to secure deluxe paperback, hardcover & box set editions at printing cost. Together, we can spark a new global literary renaissance alongside our small, independent publishing house called "The Library of Alexandria."

Thousands of years ago, the Library of Alexandria stood as a beacon of knowledge—until it was lost to history. We aim to reignite that spirit of preservation and discovery right now, in the modern age—only this time, it's accessible to all, in every language and every format.

Picture a world where every timeless classic, novel, poem, or philosophical treatise is not only available to read but also updated for today's readers—modernized, translated into any language or dialect, and ready to enjoy in any format you choose, whether that is in an eBook, audiobook, paperback, or deluxe hardcover & box set version a printing cost.

By joining our movement to rebuild the modern Library of Alexandria, you become part of an unprecedented mission to offer:

- **Unlimited Audiobook & eBook Access to the Greatest Classics of All Time**

    Instantly explore thousands of legendary works, from Plato and Shakespeare to Jane Austen and Leo Tolstoy. All are instantly ready to read or listen to, giving you a complete literary universe at your fingertips.

- **Paperback & Deluxe Editions at Printing Costs:**

    Purchase any title in a paperback, deluxe hardbound, or deluxe boxset edition at printing costs, shipped right to your doorstep. Curate your personal library of Alexandria with editions worthy of display—crafted to last, designed to captivate, and delivered straight to your door.

- **Modern translations for Contemporary Readers in all languages and dialects**

    Discover a vast selection of classics reimagined in clear, current language—no more struggling with outdated phrases or obscure references. Next to the original versions, we aim to offer translations in as many languages and dialects as possible.

    As we continue our translation efforts and add new languages, readers everywhere can connect with these works as if they were written today. By bridging linguistic divides, you're contributing to ensuring that these timeless stories become more meaningful, accessible, and inspiring for people across the globe.

- **Your Personal Library of Alexandria:**

    Over the months and years, you'll curate a unique physical archive of classics—each volume a testament to your taste, curiosity, and love of knowledge. It's not just about owning books—it's about curating a cultural legacy you'll cherish and pass down for generations to come.

- **Join a Global Literary Renaissance:**

    Your support fuels an ongoing mission: allowing us to reinvest in offering deluxe print editions (including special boxsets) at their true cost, broaden the range of available formats and translations, and extend the reach of these works to new audiences worldwide. By joining today, you're not just preserving a legacy of masterpieces; you set in motion a powerful wave of literary accessibility.

    We are more than a publisher—we're a movement, and we can't do it alone. Your support lets us scale our mission, preserving and reimagining history's greatest works for tomorrow's readers.

Become a Torchbearer of knowledge.

Thank you for picking up this book and allowing us into your literary journey. As you turn the pages, know that you're part of something larger: a global effort to keep these stories alive, share their wisdom across borders and generations, and spark a true cultural revival for the modern era.

If this resonates with you—please consider taking the next step by visiting:

www.libraryofalexandria.com

With gratitude and a shared love of knowledge,

The Modern Library of Alexandria Team

Visit:

www.libraryofalexandria.com

Or scan the code below:

www.ingramcontent.com/pod-product-compliance
Lightning Source LLC
LaVergne TN
LVHW030631080426
835512LV00021B/3448